Landmark American Speeches

Volume III : The 20th Century

Maureen Harrison & Steve Gilbert
Editors

Excellent Books
Carlsbad, California

EXCELLENT BOOKS
Post Office Box 131322
Carlsbad, CA 92013-1322

Publisher's Cataloging in Publication Data

Landmark American Speeches, Volume II: The 20th Century/
 Maureen Harrison, Steve Gilbert, editors.
  p. cm. - (Landmark Speeches Series)
Bibliography: p.

1. Speeches, addresses, etc., American.
I. Title. II. Harrison, Maureen. III. Gilbert, Steve.
IV. Series: Landmark Speeches Series.

PN6122. L235 2001   LC 98-72975
815.508 L235 -dc20   ISBN 1-880780-18-6

Introduction

Speech is power.
- Ralph Waldo Emerson

Landmark American Speeches is a collection of outstanding public eloquence, clearly spoken powerful words, that allow readers to *hear* the great words of extraordinary Americans.

The third volume of this collection, *Landmark American Speeches: The 20th Century*, presents thirty-six timeless speeches, each placed in its correct historic context by a complete biography of the speaker, a thorough history of the speech, and an extensive bibliography of the event.

In *Landmark American Speeches: The 20th Century*, the reader will find unforgettable speeches on the most important political, social, and moral issues of their times - Jane Addams on world peace - *I should like to see the women of civilization rebel against the senseless wholesale human sacrifice of warfare.* Franklin Roosevelt on World War II - *Yesterday, December 7, 1941 - a date which will live in infamy.* Martin Luther King, Jr. on brotherhood - *I have a dream my four little children will one day live in a nation where they will not be judged by the color of their skin but by the content of their character.* Betty Friedan on sisterhood - *We faced the enemy and the enemy was us.* John F. Kennedy on national sacrifice - *And so, my fellow Americans - ask not what your country can do for you - ask what you can do for your country.* César Chávez on personal sacrifice - *To be a man is to suffer for others. God help us to be men!* Barbara Jordan on patriotism - *My faith in the Constitution is whole, it is complete, it is total.* Robert F. Kennedy on freedom - *This is a Day of Affirmation - a celebration of liberty.* Ronald Reagan on faith - *Let us renew our faith.* Colin Powell on compassion - *There are still Americans who are not sharing in the American Dream.*

Edited for readers, writers, and researchers at all levels, *Landmark American Speeches* provides librarians with a right-at-their-fingertips, easy-to-access speech reference.

Landmark American Speeches: The 20ᵗʰ Century presents to the reader an unblinking view of how modern Americans viewed their world - Helen Keller - *I do not believe that there is anyone in this city of kind hearts who would willingly receive dividends if he knew that they were paid in part with blinded eyes and broken backs.* Clarence Darrow - *We are marching backward to the glorious ages of the sixteenth century when bigots burned the men who dared to bring any intelligence and enlightenment and culture to the human mind.* Carry Nation - *It is said that drink kills a man a minute.* Mother Jones - *Hear the wail of the working children.* George Wallace - *I say - Segregation now! Segregation tomorrow! Segregation forever!* Joseph McCarthy - *I have in my hand fifty-seven cases of individuals who are card-carrying members of the Communist Party.* Eugene Debs - *While there is a lower class, I am in it; while there is a criminal element, I am of it; while there is a soul in prison, I am not free.* Dwight D. Eisenhower - *We must guard against the acquisition of unwarranted influence by the military-industrial complex.* Malcolm X - *If I die in the morning, I'll die saying one thing - the ballot or the bullet.* Ryan White - *Don't give up, be proud of who you are, and never feel sorry for yourself.*

From Franklin Roosevelt's *The only thing we have to fear is fear itself* to Lou Gehrig's *Luckiest man on the face of the earth,* and from Barry Goldwater's *Extremism in the defense of liberty is no vice!* to Richard Nixon's *Checkers,* this third volume of *Landmark American Speeches* is designed to be every reader's speech reference and every librarian's speech resource.

Once a speech was selected for inclusion in *Landmark American Speeches,* the editors made every effort to either obtain the original text, or to reconcile differing texts, to provide the general adult and young adult reader the authentic words of the speakers. The only change we made to the texts is to carefully edit the essential sections presented into modern spelling and grammar.

Eloquence made Americans listen to these words. The ideas these *Landmark Speeches* contain have made them timeless.

- M.H. & S.G.

Table Of Contents

W.E.B. DuBois
Credo
22

I believe in the Negro Race, in the beauty of its genius, the sweetness of its soul, and its strength in that meekness which shall yet inherit this turbulent earth.

Albert Einstein
The War Is Won But The Peace Is Not
25

We delivered this weapon into the hands of the American and the British people as trustees of the whole of mankind, as fighters for peace and liberty.

Dwight D. Eisenhower
The Military-Industrial Complex
28

In the councils of government, we must guard against the acquisition of unwarranted influence, whether sought or unsought, by the military-industrial complex. The potential for the disastrous rise of misplaced power exists and will persist.

Betty Friedan
The Power Of Our Sisterhood
37

We faced the enemy and the enemy was us, was our own lack of self-confidence, was woman's self-denigration.

Lou Gehrig
The Luckiest Man On The Face Of The Earth
43

Fans, for the past two weeks you have been reading about a bad break I got. Yet today I consider myself the luckiest man on the face of the earth.

Barry Goldwater
Extremism In Defense Of Liberty Is No Vice
45

I would remind you that extremism in the defense of liberty is no vice. And let me remind you also that moderation in the pursuit of justice is no virtue!

Lyndon Johnson
The Tonkin Gulf
57

Aggression by terror against the peaceful villagers of South Vietnam has now been joined by open aggression on the high seas against the United States of America.

Mother Jones
The Wail Of The Children
60

We want [the President] to hear the wail of the children, who never have a chance to go to school, but work from ten to eleven hours a day in the textile mills.

Barbara Jordan
Watergate
63

My faith in the Constitution is whole, it is complete, it is total. I am not going to sit here and be an idle spectator to the diminution, the subversion, the destruction of the Constitution.

Helen Keller
The Social Causes of Blindness
70

I do not believe that there is any one in this city of kind hearts who would willingly receive dividends if he knew that they were paid in part with blinded eyes and broken backs.

Joseph McCarthy
The Witch Hunt
112

I have in my hand fifty-seven cases of individuals who would appear to be either card-carrying members or certainly loyal to the Communist Party.

Carry Nation
Thou Shalt Not Drink
118

It is said that drink kills a man a minute. Suppose that we had a war that killed a man every five minutes. Would there not be howling for an end of bloodshed? This is more than ten times worse, for the soul is more valuable than the body.

Richard Nixon
Checkers
124

The best and only answer to a smear or to an honest misunderstanding of the facts is to tell the truth. And that's why I'm here tonight. I want to tell you my side of the case.

Colin Powell
Sharing The American Dream
130

Despite more than two centuries of moral and material progress, despite all our efforts to achieve a more perfect union, there are still Americans who are not sharing in the American Dream.

Ronald Reagan
The Reagan Revolution
135

With all the creative energy at our command, let us begin an era of national renewal. Let us renew our determination, our courage, and our strength. And let us renew our faith and our hope.

Benjamin Spock
A Call To Resist Illegitimate Authority
184

We believe that every free man has a legal right and a moral duty to exert every effort to end this war.

Harry Truman
Hiroshima
189

The force from which the sun draws its power has been loosed against those who brought war to the Far East.

George Wallace
Segregation Now! Segregation Tomorrow! Segregation Forever!
195

I draw the line in the dust and toss the gauntlet before the feet of tyranny, and I say, Segregation now! Segregation tomorrow! Segregation forever!

Ryan White
I Have AIDS
199

AIDS can destroy a family if you let it, but luckily for my sister and me, Mom taught us to keep going. Don't give up, be proud of who you are, and never feel sorry for yourself.

Woodrow Wilson
The League Of Nations
204

The fortunes of mankind are now in the hands of the plain people of the whole world.

Malcolm X
The Ballot Or The Bullet
211

If I die in the morning, I'll die saying one thing - the ballot or the bullet.

Chronological Table Of Speeches

1941
Franklin D. Roosevelt
The Day That Will Live In Infamy

1945
Harry Truman *Hiroshima*

Albert Einstein *The War Is Won But The Peace Is Not*

1947
George Marshall *The Marshall Plan*

1948
Eleanor Roosevelt *Human Rights*

1950
Joseph McCarthy *The Witch Hunt*

1951
Douglas MacArthur *Old Soldiers Never Die*

1952
Richard Nixon *Checkers*

1961
Dwight D. Eisenhower
The Military-Industrial Complex

John F. Kennedy
Ask Not What Your Country Can Do For You

1963
George Wallace
*Segregation Now! Segregation Tomorrow!
Segregation Forever!*

Martin Luther King, Jr.
I Have A Dream

1964
Barry Goldwater
Extremism In Defense Of Liberty Is No Vice

Malcolm X *The Ballot Or The Bullet*

Permissions & Acknowledgments

César Chávez. Reprinted by permission of the César E. Chávez Foundation.

Albert Einstein. Permission granted by The Albert Einstein Archives, The Jewish National & University Library, The Hebrew University of Jerusalem, Israel.

Betty Friedan. Reprinted by permission of Betty Friedan.

Barry Goldwater. Reprinted by permission of Mrs. Susan Goldwater.

Barbara Jordan. The editors gratefully acknowledge the assistance of Gail Bunce of the University of Texas, Austin.

Helen Keller. Courtesy of the American Foundation for the Blind, Helen Keller Archives.

Bobby Kennedy. The editors gratefully acknowledge the assistance of the office of Senator Edward Kennedy.

Martin Luther King, Jr. Reprinted by arrangement with The Heirs to the Estate of Martin Luther King, Jr., c/o Writers House, Inc. as agent for the proprietor. Copyright 1963 by Martin Luther King, Jr., copyright renewed 1991 by Coretta Scott King.

Richard Nixon. Permission granted by the Estate of Richard Nixon. The editors also gratefully acknowledge the assistance of Susan Naulty of the Richard M. Nixon Library.

Colin Powell. Reprinted by permission of Colin Powell.

Margaret Sanger. The editors gratefully acknowledge the assistance of The Margaret Sanger Papers Project.

Benjamin Spock. Permission granted by the Executor of the Estate of Jessica Mitford.

George Wallace. The editors gratefully acknowledge the assistance of the Department of Archives and History of the State of Alabama.

Malcolm X. Copyright 1965, 1989 by Betty Shabazz and Pathfinder Press. Reprinted by permission.

This book is dedicated in loving memory to

Ethel and Leon Pattick

Jane Addams
Women And World Peace
March 12, 1932

Miss Jane Addams is the foremost woman of her nation. In honoring her with this Nobel Prize for Peace we also render homage to the work which women can do for peace and human brotherhood.
- The Nobel Peace Prize Committee, 1931

Jane Addams was born on September 6, 1860 in Cedarville, Illinois, the child of John and Sarah (Webster) Addams. Educated to be a Christian missionary, Addams formed a *simple plan* - to found an anti-poverty Settlement House. In 1889, in a poor Chicago slum neighborhood, Addams, in what she called an *effort to humanize justice,* opened Hull House to feed, clothe, and educate the poor. Addams' work on behalf of the poor made her the most famous woman in America. Her work on behalf of world peace made her the most famous woman in the world.

A lifelong pacifist opposed to all war, Jane Addams wrote, *World peace is not the absence of war but the unfolding of a process for the nurturing of human life.* In 1914, after the outbreak of Europe's *Great War*, Addams, along with other female pacifists, worked for peace. *We were,* wrote Addams, *ridiculed as "peacettes."* At the end of *The War To End All Wars*, Addams founded The Women's International League for Peace and Freedom, a permanent organization working for the abolition of war, whose peacemaking efforts she led for the next sixteen years. She wrote, *In the history of one nation after another, it was the mothers who first protested that their children should no longer be slain as living sacrifices upon the altars of warring tribal gods.*

On December 19, 1931, Jane Addams, in recognition of her work as a peacemaker, was awarded the Nobel Peace Prize. On March 12, 1932, too ill to accept her prize in person, she issued this enduring statement of her ideas and her ideals, *Women And World Peace.*

The chief skepticism pacifism meets comes from a widely accepted conviction that war is a necessary and inevitable factor in human affairs. Let us consider that in the light of one example.

. . . . At the end of [the Great War] Europe was confronted by a crisis unequaled since the Great Plague, or the famine accompanying the Thirty Years' War, when a third of the population of Europe perished. And yet, in spite of this lesson, a decade after the treaty was signed six million men were under arms in fifty-two nations; ten million were receiving military training; twenty-seven million were enrolled in military reserves! During the period immediately after the Great War closed, political leaders had turned to a more arrant and arrogant *nationalism* than that which had gone before.

We have reached a stage in the advancement of civilization when we are quite willing to concede that finance, industry, transportation, science, medicine, culture, and trade are not bounded by national frontiers, but must be international. Must our political thought alone remain insular and blindly *national?*

Surely, now that we begin to comprehend the moral, social, and economic consequences of the late war, we must examine openly the question of how to avoid another.

It seems necessary that two things be done:

First, that peaceful methods substituted for war in the settlement of international disputes should be increased and strengthened.

Second, that these peaceful methods should be given a fair chance invariably to succeed, even in grave crises, by the final abolition of armaments.

Ten or a dozen of these peaceful methods have been developed in an unprecedented degree during the past generation. The chief of these were the Hague Court of Arbitration, the League of Nations, the World Court, and the Kellogg Pact. Each of these has been used repeatedly, the first one many times; and whenever they have been resorted to they invariably have succeeded.

But in a half dozen crises of the past generation, including the Chinese-Japanese crisis of today, they have been brushed aside and a resort has been made to armed force.

At the Geneva arms conference, which at this writing is about to open, a principle should be agreed upon and rigidly applied. The nations should pledge themselves, in another Kellogg Pact, never again to resort to armaments in their dealings with one another. The next step would be to agree upon methods of securing total disarmament. Experts now conceive of the warfare of the future as bound to involve whole populations.

At the last Women's International League Congress a report on disarmament was read which stated, *Defensive warfare will have no meaning as nothing can any longer be defended; for modern war will inevitably be an attack on the civil population.*

The history of one nation after another shows that it was the mothers who first protested that their children should no longer be slain as living sacrifices upon the altars of tribal gods. Women rebelled against the waste of the life they had nurtured.

I should like to see the women of civilization rebel against the senseless wholesale human sacrifice of warfare. I am convinced that many thousands of women throughout the world would gladly rise to this challenge.

Jane Addams

Afterward

In addition to her continuing work at Hull House and the Women's International League for Peace and Freedom, Jane Addams helped found and nurture organizations promoting social justice, including The National Federation of Settlements, The National Woman's Trade Union League, The National Association for the Advancement of Colored People, The National American Woman Suffrage Association, and The American Civil Liberties Union.

Jane Addams died on May 21, 1935.

Selected Reading

Adams, Jane, *Twenty Years at Hull House*, 1910.
_____, *The Second Twenty Years at Hull House*, 1930.
Davis, Allen, *American Heroine: The Life and Legend of Jane Addams*, 1973.
Diliberto, Gioia, *A Useful Woman: The Early Life of Jane Addams*, 1999.
Farrell, John, *Beloved Lady: A History of Jane Addams' Ideas on Reform and Peace*, 1967.
Levine, Daniel, *Jane Addams and the Liberal Tradition*, 1971.
Linn, James, *Jane Addams: A Biography*, 1968.
Tims, Margaret, *Jane Addams of Hull House*, 1961.

César Chávez
The Nonviolent Struggle For Justice
March 11, 1968

How long will it be before we take seriously the importance of the workers who harvest the food we eat? **- César Chávez, 1974**

César Estrada Chávez was born near Yuma, Arizona on March 31, 1927, the child of Librado and Juana Chávez. In 1939 the Chávez family lost their farm and were forced to become migrant workers. The family made a meager living in California's Central Valley, traveling from farm to farm to pick fruits and vegetables. César was part of the family's effort from the age of 12 until 17. After his service in World War II, Chávez became a community activist in the early 1950's and a labor organizer in the early 1960's.

In 1962 Chávez formed a labor union for migrant workers, the United Farm Workers, in Delano, California, the center of the grape-growing industry. *La Causa*, Chávez's true cause, was to obtain through negotiation with the growers a living wage and better working conditions for farm workers. When the grape growers refused to negotiate with the UFW, Chávez called a strike against their vineyards. When the grape growers still refused to negotiate with the UFW, Chávez called for a nationwide boycott of their products.

In the third year of the bitter, sometimes violent, Delano Grape Strike, César Chávez, taking a page from the militant non-violent tactics of India's Mahatma Ghandi, began a highly publicized fast that lasted twenty-five days - February 15-March 11, 1968. Support for Chávez and the UFW came from many people throughout America, including Dr. Martin Luther King, Jr. and Robert F. Kennedy.

On March 11, 1968, in Delano's Public Park, César Chávez, having broken his twenty-five day fast after the grape growers agreed to negotiate, delivered this landmark speech, *The Nonviolent Struggle For Justice*.

César Chávez

Our struggle is not easy. Those who oppose our cause are rich and powerful, and they have many allies in high places. We are poor. Our allies are few. But we have something the rich do not own. We have our bodies and spirits and the justice of our cause as our weapons.

When we are honest with ourselves, we must admit that our lives are all that really belong to us. So it is how we use our lives that determines what kind of men we are. It is my deepest belief that only by giving of our lives do we find life.

I am convinced that the truest act of courage, the strongest act of manliness, is to sacrifice ourselves for others in a totally nonviolent struggle for justice. To be a man is to suffer for others. God help us to be men!

Afterward
On July 29, 1970, the Grape Growers and the United Farm Workers signed a contract, ending the Delano Grape Strike. Chávez spent the rest of his life fighting for *La Causa*.

César Chávez died on April 23, 1993.

Selected Reading
Collins, David R., *Farmworker's Friend: The Story of César Chávez*, 1996.
Day, Mark, *César Chávez and the Farm Workers*, 1971.
Ferriss, Susan, and Ricardo Sandoval, *The Fight in the Fields: César Chávez and the Farmworkers' Movement*, 1997.
Fusco, Paul, *La Causa: The California Grape Strike*, 1970.
Meister, Dick, and Anne Loftis, *A Long Time Coming*, 1977.
Pitrone, Jean M., *Chávez, Man of the Migrants*, 1971.
Rodriguez, Consuelo, *César Chávez*, 1991.
Taylor, Ronald, *Chávez and the Farm Workers*, 1975.
Zannos, Susan, *César Chávez*, 1999.

Bill Clinton
The Oklahoma City Bombing
April 23, 1995

*Our Plan: We drive a truck into the FBI Building and blow it up.
We can wreak havoc. Several hundred people will be killed.*
-Andrew McDonald, *The Turner Diaries*, 1978

The Turner Diaries, a fictional account of a militant right
wing revolution against the United States Government, has
reportedly sold over 200,000 copies. One of those copies
belonged to twenty-seven-year-old Timothy McVeigh.

In 1995 Oklahoma City's Alfred P. Murrah Federal Building
housed the offices of the Federal Bureau of Investigation,
the U.S. Secret Service, the Drug Enforcement Administration, the Bureau of Alcohol, Tobacco, and Firearms, the
Social Security Administration, the Veterans Administration, the U.S. Army, the U.S. Marines, and a child care center.

At 9:02 a.m. on April 19, 1995, a truck bomb (2,000 pounds
of explosives) was detonated outside the Federal Building,
killing 168 people, including 19 children, and injuring over
500. The picture of a firefighter carrying the body of a
dead child out of the rubble exemplified the horror.

The bombing, the worst act of domestic terrorism ever
committed, was carried out by Timothy McVeigh as his personal retaliation against the United States Government for
the catastrophic end to the FBI/Branch Davidian Waco
Siege. On that date, April 19, 1993, McVeigh swore venge-
ance, writing, *Blood will flow in the streets.*

On April 23, 1995, in Oklahoma City, a memorial was held.
The Reverend Billy Graham said, *The blast was like a violent
explosion ripping at the heart of America. Long after the rubble is
cleared, the scars of this senseless and evil outrage will remain.* President Bill Clinton, in a effort to begin the healing, gave this
emotional landmark speech, *The Oklahoma City Bombing.*

7

I am honored to be here today to represent the American people. But I have to tell you that Hillary and I also come as parents, as husband and wife, as people who were your neighbors for some of the best years of our lives.

Today our Nation joins with you in grief. We mourn with you. We share your hope against hope that some may still survive. We thank all those who have worked so heroically to save lives and to solve this crime, those here in Oklahoma, and those who are all across this great land, and many who left their own lives to come here to work hand in hand with you.

We pledge to do all we can to help you heal the injured, to rebuild this city, and to bring to justice those who did this evil.

This terrible sin took the lives of our American family - innocent children, in that building only because their parents were trying to be good parents as well as good workers; citizens in the building going about their daily business; and many there who served the rest of us, who worked to help the elderly and the disabled, who worked to support our farmers and our veterans, who worked to enforce our laws and to protect us. Let us say clearly - they served us well, and we are grateful. But for so many of you they were also neighbors and friends. You saw them at church or the PTA meetings, at the civic clubs, at the ball park. You know them in ways that all the rest of America could not.

And to all the members of the families here present who have suffered loss - though we share your grief, your pain is unimaginable, and we know that. We cannot undo it. That is God's work.

Our words seem small beside the loss you have endured. But I found a few I wanted to share today. I've received a lot of letters in these last terrible days. One stood out because it came from a young widow and a mother of three whose own husband was murdered with over 200 other Americans when Pan Am 103 was shot down. Here is what that woman said I should say to you today,

The anger you feel is valid, but you must not allow yourselves to be consumed by it. The hurt you feel must not be allowed to turn into hate, but instead into the search for justice. The loss you feel must not paralyze your own lives. Instead, you must try to pay tribute to your loved ones by continuing to do all the things they left undone, thus ensuring they did not die in vain.

Wise words from one who also knows.

You have lost too much, but you have not lost everything. And you have certainly not lost America, for we will stand with you for as many tomorrows as it takes.

If ever we needed evidence of that, I could only recall the words of Governor and Mrs. Keating. If anybody thinks that Americans are mostly mean and selfish, they ought to come to Oklahoma. If anybody thinks Americans have lost the capacity for love and caring and courage, they ought to come to Oklahoma.

To all my fellow Americans beyond this hall I say - one thing we owe those who have sacrificed is the duty to purge ourselves of the dark forces which gave rise to this evil. They are forces that threaten our common peace, our freedom, our way of life.

Let us teach our children that the God of comfort is also the God of righteousness. Those who trouble their own house will inherit the wind. Justice will prevail.

Let us let our own children know that we will stand against the forces of fear. When there is talk of hatred, let us stand up and talk against it. When there is talk of violence, let us stand up and talk against it. In the face of death, let us honor life. As St. Paul admonished us, let us not be overcome by evil, but overcome evil with good.

Yesterday Hillary and I had the privilege of speaking with some children of other Federal employees, children like those who were lost here. And one little girl said something we will never forget. She said we should all plant a tree in memory of the children. So this morning before we got on the plane to come here, at the White House, we planted that tree in honor of the children of Oklahoma. It was a dogwood with its wonderful spring flower and its deep, enduring roots. It embodies the lesson of the Psalms that the life of a good person is like a tree whose leaf does not wither.

My fellow Americans, a tree takes a long time to grow, and wounds take a long time to heal. But we must begin. Those who are lost now belong to God. Some day we will be with them. But until that happens, their legacy must be our lives.

Thank you all, and God bless you.

Bill Clinton

Afterward

Timothy McVeigh was arrested on April 19, 1995. Tried and convicted for mass murder, he has been sentenced to death. The site of the Oklahoma City Bombing is now a permanent memorial to its victims.

Selected Reading

Jones, Stephen, and Peter Israel, *Others Unknown: The Oklahoma City Bombing Case and Conspiracy*, 1998.

Kight, Marsha, *Forever Changed: Remembering Oklahoma City*, 1998.

Maraniss, David, *First in His Class: A Biography of Bill Clinton*, 1995.

Ross, Jim, and Paul Myers, Editors, *We Will Never Forget: Eyewitness Accounts of the Bombing of the Oklahoma City Federal Building*, 1996.

Serrano, Richard, *One Of Ours: Timothy McVeigh and the Oklahoma City Bombing*, 1998.

Clarence Darrow
In Defense Of John T. Scopes
July 21, 1925

It shall be unlawful for any teacher in a public school to teach any theory that denies Divine Creation of man as taught in the Bible, and to teach instead that man has descended from lower animals.
- Tennessee's Anti-Evolution Teaching Law, 1925

In 1859 naturalist Charles Darwin published *The Origin of Species*, offering the theory of evolution as a scientific proof that man was descended from lower life forms. This was in direct conflict with the literal biblical account of creation.

On March 21, 1925, Tennessee became the first state to enact an Anti-Evolution Law, called by opponents a *Monkey Law*. It prohibited the teaching of evolution in the public schools. John T. Scopes, a high school biology teacher in Dayton, Tennessee, was charged with its violation.

William Jennings Bryan, a statesman, politician, and evangelist, who had urged Bible Belt states, including Tennessee, to enact such Anti-Evolution Laws, volunteered to aid the prosecution. To defend Scopes, the American Civil Liberties Union hired the most famous criminal defense lawyer in America - Clarence Darrow.

Clarence Seward Darrow was born on April 18, 1857 in Kinsman, Ohio, the child of Amirus and Emily (Eddy) Darrow. Admitted to practice in 1878, Darrow won fame for defending, and saving, unpopular defendants in hopeless cases - socialist leader Eugene Debs in 1894, labor leader Bill Hayward in 1908, *thrill-killers* Leopold and Loeb in 1924, and architect Frank Lloyd Wright in 1926.

On July 21, 1925, the Scopes Monkey Trial, which featured the famous cross-examination of William Jennings Bryan by Darrow, ended with this landmark speech to the jury by Clarence Darrow, *In Defense of John T. Scopes*.

Clarence Darrow

If the teaching of evolution is the subject of a criminal act, then it cannot make a criminal out of a teacher in the public schools and leave a man free to teach it in a private school. It cannot make it criminal for a teacher in the public schools to teach evolution, and for the same man to stand among the hustings and teach it. It cannot make it a criminal act for this teacher to teach evolution, and permit books upon evolution to be sold in every store in the state of Tennessee and to permit the newspapers from foreign cities to bring into your peaceful community the horrible utterances of evolution. Oh, no, nothing like that. If the state of Tennessee has any force in this day of fundamentalism, in this day when religious bigotry and hatred is being kindled all over our land, see what can be done?

. . . . To strangle puppies is good when they grow up into mad dogs, maybe. I will tell you what is going to happen - and I do not pretend to be a prophet - but I do not need to be a prophet to know. Your Honor knows the fires that have been lighted in America to kindle religious bigotry and hate. You can take judicial notice of them if you cannot of anything else. You know that there is no suspicion which possesses the minds of men like bigotry and ignorance and hatred.

If today you can take a thing like evolution and make it a crime to teach it in the public school, tomorrow you can make it a crime to teach it in the private school, and the next year you can make it a crime to teach it from the hustings or in the church. At the next session you may ban books and the newspapers. Soon you may set Catholic against Protestant and Protestant against Protestant, and try to foist your own religion upon the minds of men. If you can do one you can do the other.

Ignorance and fanaticism is ever busy and needs feeding. Always it is feeding and gloating for more. Today it is the public school teachers, tomorrow the private. The next day the preachers and the lecturers, the magazines, the books, the newspapers. After a while, Your Honor, it is the setting of man against man and creed against creed until, with flying banners and beating drums, we are marching backward to the glorious ages of the sixteenth century, when bigots lighted fagots to burn the men who dared to bring any intelligence and enlightenment and culture to the human mind.

Afterward

John T. Scopes was found guilty of violating Tennessee's *Monkey Law* and was fined $100. In 1967 Tennessee repealed the 1925 Anti-Evolution Law.

Clarence Darrow died on March 13, 1938.

Selected Reading

Darrow, Clarence, *The Story Of My Life*, 1996.
Harrison, Charles Y., *Clarence Darrow*, 1931.
Hynd, Alan, *Defenders of the Damned*, 1960.
Livingston, John C., *Clarence Darrow: The Mind of a Sentimental Rebel*, 1988.
Sayer, James E., *Clarence Darrow: Public Advocate*, 1978.
Stone, Irving, *Clarence Darrow For the Defense, A Biography*, 1941.
Tierney, Kevin, *Darrow, A Biography*, 1979.
Weinberg, Arthur, *Attorney For The Damned*, 1957.
_____, and Lila Weinberg, *Clarence Darrow: A Sentimental Rebel*, 1980.

Movies:
Inherit The Wind, 1960.

Eugene Debs
The Gospel Of Socialism
September 14, 1918

I am for Socialism because I am for humanity. - **Eugene Debs**

Eugene Victor Debs was born on November 5, 1855 in Terre Haute, Indiana, the child of Jean Daniel and Marguerite (Bettrich) Debs. In 1895 Debs, President of the American Railway Union, was jailed for leading a nationwide rail strike. *Strikes,* said Debs, *are the last means which are resorted to by men driven to desperation after all peaceful efforts to obtain justice have failed.* Debs filled his jail time by studying socialism, the economic theory that government, not private enterprise, should own and manage the means of production and distribution of goods and services. In 1898 Eugene Debs founded the Socialist Party of America and spent the rest of his life speaking and working on behalf of socialism.

On June 15, 1917, after America's entry into World War I, Congress enacted The Espionage Act, which curtailed free speech in wartime. On June 16, 1918, speaking in Canton, Ohio at an anti-war rally, Eugene Debs said, *They tell us that we live in a great free republic - that our institutions are democratic - that we are a free and self-governing people. This is too much even for a joke.* The U.S. Justice Department charged Debs' speech was *a willful attempt to incite disloyalty,* a violation of The Espionage Act. The trial of Eugene Debs began on September 9, 1918 in Cleveland, Ohio. Debs, in his own defense, addressed the jury - *George Washington, Thomas Paine, John Adams - these were the rebels of their day. If the American Revolution had failed, the Revolutionary fathers would have been executed as felons. But it did not fail. Revolutions have a habit of succeeding when the time comes for them.* The jury returned a guilty verdict.

On September 14, 1918, in reply to the Judge's question, *Have you anything further to say on your behalf before the Court passes sentence on you?,* Eugene Debs made this landmark speech, *The Gospel of Socialism.*

Your Honor, years ago I recognized my kinship with all living beings, and I made up my mind that I was not one bit better than the meanest of earth. I said then - I say now - that while there is a lower class, I am in it; while there is a criminal element, I am of it; while there is a soul in prison, I am not free.

If the law under which I have been convicted is a good law, then there is no reason why sentence should not be pronounced upon me. I listened to all that was said in this court in support and justification of this law, but my mind remains unchanged. I look upon it as a despotic enactment in flagrant conflict with democratic principles and with the spirit of free institutions.

. . . . Your Honor, I have stated in this court that I am opposed to the form of our present government, that I am opposed to the social system in which we live, that I believed in the change of both - but by perfectly peaceable and orderly means.

Let me call your attention to the fact this morning that in this system five percent of our people own and control two-thirds of our wealth; sixty-five percent of the people, embracing the working class who produce all wealth, have but five percent to show for it.

. . . . In the struggle - the unceasing struggle - between the toilers and producers and their exploiters, I have tried, as best I might, to serve those among whom I was born, with whom I expect to share my lot until the end of my days.

I am thinking this morning of the men in the mills and factories; I am thinking of the women who, for a paltry wage, are compelled to work out their lives; of the little children who, in this system, are robbed of their childhood, and in their early, tender years, are seized in the remorseless grasp of Mammon, and forced into the industrial dungeons, there to feed the machines while they themselves are being starved body and soul. I can see them dwarfed, diseased, stunted, their little lives broken, and their hopes blasted, because in this high noon of our twentieth century civilization, money is still so much more important than human life. Gold is god and rules in the affairs of men.

The little girls, and there are a million of them in this country - this the most favored land beneath the bending skies, a land in which we have vast areas of rich and fertile soil, material resources in inexhaustible abundance, the most marvelous productive machinery on earth, millions of eager workers ready to apply their labor to that machinery to produce an abundance for every man, woman, and child and if there are still many millions of our people who are the victims of poverty, whose life is a ceaseless struggle all the way from youth to age, until at last death comes to their rescue and stills the aching heart, and lulls the victim to dreamless sleep, it is not the fault of the Almighty - it can't be charged to nature - it is due entirely to an outgrown social system that ought to be abolished not only in the interest of the working class, but in a higher interest of all humanity.

When I think of these little children - the girls that are in the textile mills of all description in the East, in the cotton factories of the South - when I think of them at work in a vitiated atmosphere, when I think of them at work when they ought to be at play or at school, when I think that when they do grow up, if they live long enough to approach the marriage state, they are unfit for it. Their nerves are worn out, their tissue is exhausted, their vitality is spent. They have been fed to industry. Their lives have been coined into gold. Their offspring are born tired. That is why there are so many failures in our modern life.

Your Honor, the five percent of the people that I have made reference to constitute that element that absolutely rules our country. They privately own all our public necessities. They wear no crowns; they wield no scepters; they sit upon no thrones; and yet they are our economic masters and our political rulers. They control this government and all of its institutions. They control the courts.

. . . . The five percent of our people who own and control all the sources of wealth, all of the nation's industries, all of the means of our common life, it is they who declare war; it is they who make peace; it is they who control our destiny. And so long as this is true, we can make no just claim to being a democratic government, a self-governing people.

I believe, Your Honor, in common with all Socialists, that this nation ought to own and control its industries. I believe, as all Socialists do, that all things that are jointly needed and used ought to be jointly owned - that industry, the basis of life, instead of being the private property of the few and operated for their enrichment, ought to be the common property of all, democratically administered in the interest of all.

John D. Rockefeller has today an income of sixty million dollars a year, five million dollars a month, two hundred thousand dollars a day. He does not produce a penny of it. I make no attack upon Mr. Rockefeller personally. I do not in the least dislike him. If he were in need and it were in my power to serve him, I should serve him as gladly as I would any other human being. I have no quarrel with Mr. Rockefeller personally, nor with any other capitalist. I am simply opposing a social order in which it is possible for one man who does absolutely nothing that is useful to amass a fortune of hundreds of millions of dollars, while millions of men and women who work all of the days of their lives secure barely enough for an existence.

This order of things cannot always endure. I have registered my protest against it. I recognize the feebleness of my effort, but, fortunately, I am not alone. There are multiplied thousands of others who, like myself, have come to realize that before we may truly enjoy the blessings of civilized life, we must reorganize society upon a mutual and cooperative basis; and to this end we have organized a great economic and political movement that is spread over the face of all the earth.

There are today upwards of sixty million Socialists - loyal, devoted, adherents to this cause, regardless of nationality, race, creed, color, or sex. They are all making common cause. They are all spreading the propaganda of the new social order. They are waiting, watching, and working through all the weary hours of the day and night. They are still in the minority. They have learned how to be patient and abide their time. They feel - they know, indeed - that the time is coming, in spite of all opposition, all persecution, when this emancipating gospel will spread among all the peoples, and when this minority will become the triumphant majority, and sweeping into power, inaugurate the greatest change in history.

In that day we will have the universal commonwealth - not the destruction of the nation, but, on the contrary, the harmonious cooperation of every nation with every other nation on earth. In that day, war will curse this earth no more.

I have been accused, Your Honor, of being an enemy of the soldier. I hope I am laying no flattering unction to my soul when I say that I don't believe the soldier has a more sympathetic friend than I am. If I had my way there would be no soldiers. But I realize the sacrifices they are making, Your Honor. I can think of them. I can feel for them. I can sympathize with them. That is one of the reasons why I have been doing what little has been in my power to bring about a condition of affairs in this country worthy of the sacrifices they have made and that they are now making in its behalf.

. . . . Your Honor, I ask no mercy; I plead for no immunity. I realize that finally the right must prevail. I never more clearly comprehended than now the great struggle between the powers of greed on the one hand and upon the other the rising hosts of freedom. I can see the dawn of a better day of humanity. The people are awakening. In due course of time, they will come into their own.

When the mariner, sailing over tropic seas, looks for relief from his weary watch, he turns his eyes toward the Southern Cross, burning luridly above the tempest-vexed ocean. As the midnight approaches, the Southern Cross begins to bend, and the whirling worlds change their places, and with starry finger-points the Almighty marks the passage of Time upon the dial of the universe; and though no bell may beat the glad tidings, the look-out knows that the midnight is passing, that relief and rest are close at hand.

Let the people take heart and hope everywhere, for the cross is bending, the midnight is passing, and joy cometh with the morning.

Eugene Debs

He is true to God who is true to man.
Wherever wrong is done
To the humblest and the weakest
'Neath the all-beholding sun,
That wrong is also done to us,
And they are slaves most base
Whose love of right is for themselves
And not for all the race.

Your Honor, I thank you, and I thank all of this court for their courtesy, for their kindness, which I shall remember always. I am prepared to receive your sentence.

Afterward

Eugene Debs, then sixty-three years old, was sentenced to ten years imprisonment in a federal penitentiary. On December 25, 1921, President Warren G. Harding commuted his sentence.

Eugene Debs died on October 20, 1926.

Selected Reading

Coleman, McAlister, *Eugene V. Debs, A Man Unafraid*, 1975.
Currie, Harold W., *Eugene V. Debs*, 1976.
Debs, Eugene, *Debs: His Life, Writing and Speeches*, 1908.
_____, *Walls and Bars*, 1973.
Ginger, Ray, *The Bending Cross: A Biography of Eugene Victor Debs*, 1992.
Karsner, David, *Debs: His Authorized Life and Letters*, 1919.
Morais, Herbert M., and William Cahn, *Gene Debs: The Story of a Fighting American*, 1948.
Radosh, Ronald, *Debs*, 1971.
Salvatore, Nick, *Eugene Debs: Citizen and Socialist*, 1982.
Schnittkind, Henry T., *The Story of Eugene Debs*, 1929.
Young, Marguerite, *Harp Song for a Radical: The Life and Times of Eugene Debs*, 1999.

W.E.B. DuBois
Credo
October 6, 1904

I am by birth and law a free black American citizen. Boldly and without flinching, I will face the hard fact that in this, my own country, I must expect insult and discrimination . . . but may God forget me if at any time I ever weakly admit to myself or to the world that wrong is not wrong, that insult is not insult, or that color discrimination is not color discrimination.

- W.E.B. DuBois, *The Crisis*, January 1913

William Edward Burghardt DuBois, the leading African American spokesman of his time, was born on February 23, 1868 in Great Barrington, Massachusetts, the child of Alfred and Mary (Silvina) DuBois. Educated at Harvard University (Ph.D., 1895), DuBois' doctoral thesis, *The Suppression of the African Slave Trade*, won him recognition as a scholar of African American history. DuBois published the first socio-economic studies of African American communities in the urban North and rural South (*The Philadelphia Negro* in 1899 and *The Negroes of Farmville, Virginia* in 1900). In 1903 he published his most famous work, a book of essays, *The Souls of Black Folk*, prophetically writing, *The problem of the twentieth century is the problem of the color line.*

A scholar by training, W.E.B. DuBois became a civil rights leader by necessity. In response to racial violence (in 1901 99 African Americans were lynched), and *legal* discrimination (the spread of southern *Jim Crow* laws), DuBois helped found an organization to work for enforceable civil rights laws - The National Association for the Advancement of Colored People. As editor of the NAACP's monthly journal, *The Crisis*, DuBois became the full-time voice, and sometime conscience, of the African American community.

On October 6, 1904, *Credo*, W.E.B. DuBois' landmark statement of his own personal and heartfelt beliefs, was delivered for the first time in Atlanta, Georgia.

I believe in God, who made of one blood all nations that on earth do dwell. I believe that all men, black and brown and white, are brothers, varying through time and opportunity, in form and gift and feature, but differing in no essential particular, and alike in soul and the possibility of infinite development.

Especially do I believe in the Negro race, in the beauty of its genius, the sweetness of its soul, and its strength in that meekness which shall yet inherit this turbulent earth.

I believe in pride of race and lineage and self, in pride of self so deep as to scorn injustice to other selves, in pride of lineage so great as to despise no man's father, in pride of race so chivalrous as neither to offer bastardy to the weak nor beg wedlock of the strong, knowing that men may be brothers in Christ, even though they be not brothers in law.

I believe in service, humble, reverent service, from the blackening of boots to the whitening of souls, for work is Heaven, idleness Hell, and wage is the *Well done!* of the Master, who summoned all them that labor and are heavy laden, making no distinction between the black, sweating cotton hands of Georgia and the first families of Virginia, since all distinction not based on deed is devilish and not divine.

I believe in the Devil and his angels, who wantonly work to narrow the opportunity of struggling human beings, especially if they be black, who spit in the faces of the fallen, strike them that cannot strike again, believe the worst and work to prove it, hating the image which their Maker stamped on a brother's soul.

I believe in the Prince of Peace. I believe that war is murder. I believe that armies and navies are at bottom the tinsel and braggadocio of oppression and wrong, and I believe that the wicked conquest of weaker and darker nations by nations whiter and stronger but foreshadows the death of that strength.

I believe in liberty for all men, the space to stretch their arms and their souls, the right to breathe and the right to vote, the freedom to choose their friends, enjoy the sunshine, and ride on the railroads, uncursed by color, thinking, dreaming, working as they will in a kingdom of beauty and love.

I believe in the training of children, black even as white, the leading out of little souls into the green pastures and beside the still waters, not for self nor peace, but for life lit by some large vision of beauty and goodness and truth, lest we forget, and the sons of the fathers, like Esau, for mere meat barter their birthright in a mighty nation.

Finally, I believe in patience, patience with the weakness of the weak and the strength of the strong, the prejudice of the ignorant and the ignorance of the blind, patience with the tardy triumph of joy and the mad chastening of sorrow, patience with God!

Afterward
W.E.B. DuBois wrote, spoke, and worked for civil rights throughout his life. He died on August 27, 1963.

Selected Reading

Aptheker, Herbert, Editor, *The Complete Published Works of W.E.B. DuBois,* 1982.

DuBois, W.E.B., *The Autobiography of W.E.B. DuBois,* 1968.

Franklin, Robert M., *Liberating Visions: Human Fulfillment and Social Justice in African-American Thought,* 1990.

Lewis, David, *W.E.B. DuBois: Biography of a Race, 1896-1919,* 1993.

Albert Einstein
The War Is Won But The Peace Is Not
December 10, 1945

[The Theory of Relativity] may make it possible to set up a nuclear chain reaction in a large mass of uranium, by which vast amounts of energy would be generated. This new phenomenon could lead to the construction of an extremely powerful bomb.

- Albert Einstein's Letter to President Roosevelt, 1939

On October 17, 1933, Albert Einstein, a German-born Jewish scientist, arrived in the United States. Einstein, acknowledged as the world's leading theoretical physicist, had, in his 1905 *Specific Theory of Relativity*, revolutionized the laws of physics as set down 300 years earlier by Sir Isaac Newton. According to the Einstein Equation ($E=mc^2$ - energy equals mass times the speed of light squared), if the atom could be split, an enormous amount of atomic energy would be released. The Atomic Age was about to be born.

Albert Einstein was born in Ulm, Germany on March 14, 1879, the child of Hermann and Pauline (Koch) Einstein. Educated as a mathematician at Swiss Polytechnic Institute, and as a theoretical physicist at the University of Zurich, Einstein published *The Special Theory of Relativity* in 1905, *The General Theory of Relativity* in 1915, *The Unified Field Theory* in 1922, and the *Quantum Theory* in 1923. For his work he was awarded the Nobel Prize in Physics.

In 1933, fleeing Nazi Germany, Einstein immigrated to the United States. In 1939, with war imminent, Einstein wrote to President Roosevelt about the possibility of creating a project to build an atomic bomb. The result was *The Manhattan Project*'s atomic bombs, which destroyed Hiroshima and Nagasaki, ending the Second World War.

On December 10, 1945, at a Nobel Prize Dinner held in New York City, Albert Einstein delivered this landmark speech, *The War Is Won But The Peace Is Not.*

Physicists find themselves in a position not unlike that of Alfred Nobel. Alfred Nobel invented the most powerful explosive ever known up to his time, a means of destruction par excellence. In order to atone for this, in order to relieve his human conscience, he instituted his awards for the promotion of peace and for achievements of peace. Today, the physicists who participated in forging the most formidable and dangerous weapon of all times are harassed by an equal feeling of responsibility, not to say guilt. And we cannot desist from warning, and warning again - we cannot and should not slacken in our efforts to make the nations of the world, and especially their governments, aware of the unspeakable disaster they are certain to provoke unless they change their attitude toward each other and toward the task of shaping the future. We helped in creating this new weapon in order to prevent the enemies of mankind from achieving it ahead of us, which, given the mentality of the Nazis, would have meant inconceivable destruction and the enslavement of the rest of the world. We delivered this weapon into the hands of the American and the British people as trustees of the whole of mankind, as fighters for peace and liberty. But so far we fail to see any guarantee of peace - we do not see any guarantee of the freedoms that were promised to the nations in the Atlantic Charter. The war is won, but the peace is not. The great powers, united in fighting, are now divided over the peace settlements. The world was promised freedom from fear, but in fact fear has increased tremendously since the termination of the war. The world was promised freedom from want, but large parts of the world are faced with starvation while others are living in abundance. The nations were promised liberation and justice. But we have witnessed, and are witnessing even now, the sad spectacle of *liberating* armies firing into populations who want their independence and social equality, and supporting in those countries, by force of arms, such parties and personalities as appear to be most suited to serve vested interests. Territorial questions and arguments of power, obsolete though they are, still prevail over the essential demands of common welfare and justice. . . .

The picture of our postwar world is not bright. As far as we, the physicists, are concerned, we are no politicians, and it has never been our wish to meddle in politics. But we know a few things that the politicians do not know. And we feel the duty to speak up and to remind those responsible that there is no escape into easy comforts, there is no distance ahead for proceeding little by little and delaying the necessary changes into an indefinite future, there is no time left for petty bargaining. The situation calls for a courageous effort, for a radical change in our whole attitude, in the entire political concept. May the spirit that prompted Alfred Nobel to create his great institution, the spirit of trust and confidence, of generosity and brotherhood among men, prevail in the minds of those upon whose decisions our destiny rests. Otherwise human civilization will be doomed.

Afterward

In 1925, accepting a prize from the British Royal Astronomical Society, Einstein wrote, *He who finds a thought that lets us penetrate even a little deeper into the eternal mystery of nature has been granted a little grace.*

Albert Einstein died on April 18, 1955.

Selected Reading

Brian, Denis, *Einstein: A Life*, 1996.
Clark, Ronald, *Einstein: The Life and Times*, 1971.
Fölsing, Albrecht, *Albert Einstein*, 1997.
French, A.P., Editor, *Einstein: A Centenary Volume*, 1979.
Highfield, Roger, *The Private Lives of Albert Einstein*, 1994.

Dwight D. Eisenhower
The Military-Industrial Complex
January 17, 1961

During the years of my Presidency, and especially the later years, I began to feel more and more uneasiness about the effect on the nation of tremendous peacetime military expenditures. . . . The idea of making a final address as President to the nation seemed to call on me to warn the nation of the danger in these developments.
- Dwight David Eisenhower, *Waging Peace*, 1965

Dwight David Eisenhower, who was known world-wide as *Ike*, was born on October 14, 1890 in Denison, Texas, the child of David and Ida (Stover) Eisenhower. Educated at the U.S. Military Academy at West Point, Dwight Eisenhower spent almost his entire adult life in service to America - 1915-1948 in the United States Army and 1952-1960 as President of the United States.

During the Second World War, General Douglas MacArthur called Dwight Eisenhower *the best officer in the U.S. Army*. Eisenhower was appointed by President Roosevelt to serve as Supreme Allied Commander. He successfully planned and led the June 6, 1944 D-Day Invasion and the battles that led to the May 7, 1945 unconditional surrender of Nazi Germany. General George C. Marshall wrote, *You have completed your mission with the greatest victory in the history of warfare.* Eisenhower went on to serve as U.S. Army Chief-of-Staff and the Supreme Commander of NATO. In 1952 he was elected, and in 1956 re-elected, President of the United States. During the last years of his Presidency, the U.S. Military and the defense industry began to plan for a Cold War military build-up that would cost hundreds of billions of dollars. President Eisenhower grew concerned.

On the night of January 17, 1961, President Eisenhower, troubled over these planned peacetime military expenditures, delivered this landmark Farewell Address, warning the nation of the danger of *The Military-Industrial Complex*.

Dwight D. Eisenhower

My fellow Americans, three days from now, after half a century in the service of our country, I shall lay down the responsibilities of office as, in traditional and solemn ceremony, the authority of the Presidency is vested in my successor.

This evening I come to you with a message of leave-taking and farewell, and to share a few final thoughts with you, my countrymen.

Like every other citizen, I wish the new President, and all who will labor with him, Godspeed. I pray that the coming years will be blessed with peace and prosperity for all.

Our people expect their President and the Congress to find essential agreement on issues of great moment, the wise resolution of which will better shape the future of the Nation.

My own relations with the Congress - which began on a remote and tenuous basis when, long ago, a member of the Senate appointed me to West Point - have since ranged to the intimate during the war and immediate post-war period and, finally, to the mutually interdependent during these past eight years.

In this final relationship, the Congress and the Administration have, on most vital issues, cooperated well to serve the national good rather than mere partisanship, and so have assured that the business of the Nation should go forward. So, my official relationship with the Congress ends in a feeling, on my part, of gratitude that we have been able to do so much together.

We now stand ten years past the midpoint of a century that has witnessed four major wars among great nations. Three of these involved our own country. Despite these holo causts, America is today the strongest, the most influential, and most productive nation in the world. Understandably proud of this preeminence, we yet realize that America's leadership and prestige depend, not merely upon our unmatched material progress, riches, and military strength, but on how we use our power in the interests of world peace and human betterment.

Throughout America's adventure in free government, our basic purposes have been to keep the peace, to foster progress in human achievement, and to enhance liberty, dignity, and integrity among people and among nations. To strive for less would be unworthy of a free and religious people. Any failure traceable to arrogance, or our lack of comprehension or readiness to sacrifice, would inflict upon us grievous hurt both at home and abroad.

Progress toward these noble goals is persistently threatened by the conflict now engulfing the world. It commands our whole attention, absorbs our very beings. We face a hostile ideology - global in scope, atheistic in character, ruthless in purpose, and insidious in method. Unhappily the danger it poses promises to be of indefinite duration. To meet it successfully, there is called for, not so much the emotional and transitory sacrifices of crisis, but rather those which enable us to carry forward steadily, surely, and without complaint the burdens of a prolonged and complex struggle - with liberty the stake. Only thus shall we remain, despite every provocation, on our charted course toward permanent peace and human betterment.

Crises there will continue to be. In meeting them, whether foreign or domestic, great or small, there is a recurring temptation to feel that some spectacular and costly action could become the miraculous solution to all current difficulties. A huge increase in newer elements of our defense -

development of unrealistic programs to cure every ill in agriculture, a dramatic expansion in basic and applied research - these and many other possibilities, each possibly promising in itself, may be suggested as the only way to the road we wish to travel.

But each proposal must be weighed in the light of a broader consideration - the need to maintain balance in and among national programs - balance between the private and the public economy, balance between cost and hoped for advantage, balance between the clearly necessary and the comfortably desirable, balance between our essential requirements as a nation and the duties imposed by the nation upon the individual, balance between actions of the moment and the national welfare of the future. Good judgment seeks balance and progress; lack of it eventually finds imbalance and frustration.

The record of many decades stands as proof that our people and their government have, in the main, understood these truths and have responded to them well, in the face of stress and threat. But threats, new in kind or degree, constantly arise. I mention two only.

A vital element in keeping the peace is our military establishment. Our arms must be mighty, ready for instant action, so that no potential aggressor may be tempted to risk his own destruction.

Our military organization today bears little relation to that known by any of my predecessors in peacetime, or indeed by the fighting men of World War II or Korea.

Until the latest of our world conflicts, the United States had no armaments industry. American makers of plowshares could, with time and as required, make swords as well. But now we can no longer risk emergency improvisation of national defense; we have been compelled to create a permanent armaments industry of vast proportions. Added to this, three and a half million men and women are directly engaged in the defense establishment. We annually spend on military security more than the net income of all United States corporations.

This conjunction of an immense military establishment and a large arms industry is new in the American experience. The total influence - economic, political, even spiritual - is felt in every city, every State house, every office of the Federal government. We recognize the imperative need for this development. Yet we must not fail to comprehend its grave implications. Our toil, resources and livelihood are all involved; so is the very structure of our society.

In the councils of government, we must guard against the acquisition of unwarranted influence, whether sought or unsought, by the military-industrial complex. The potential for the disastrous rise of misplaced power exists and will persist.

We must never let the weight of this combination endanger our liberties or democratic processes. We should take nothing for granted. Only an alert and knowledgeable citizenry can compel the proper meshing of the huge industrial and military machinery of defense with our peaceful methods and goals, so that security and liberty may prosper together.

Akin to, and largely responsible for, the sweeping changes in our industrial-military posture has been the technological revolution during recent decades.

In this revolution, research has become central; it also becomes more formalized, complex, and costly. A steadily increasing share is conducted for, by, or at the direction of, the Federal government.

Today, the solitary inventor, tinkering in his shop, has been overshadowed by task forces of scientists in laboratories and testing fields. In the same fashion, the free university, historically the fountainhead of free ideas and scientific discovery, has experienced a revolution in the conduct of research. Partly because of the huge costs involved, a government contract becomes virtually a substitute for intellectual curiosity. For every old blackboard, there are now hundreds of new electronic computers.

The prospect of domination of the nation's scholars by Federal employment, project allocations, and the power of money is ever present - and is gravely to be regarded.

Yet, in holding scientific research and discovery in respect, as we should, we must also be alert to the equal and opposite danger that public policy could itself become the captive of a scientific-technological elite.

It is the task of statesmanship to mold, to balance, and to integrate these and other forces, new and old, within the principles of our democratic system - ever aiming toward the supreme goals of our free society.

Another factor in maintaining balance involves the element of time. As we peer into society's future, we - you and I, and our government - must avoid the impulse to live only for today, plundering for our own ease and convenience the precious resources of tomorrow. We cannot mortgage the material assets of our grandchildren without risking the loss also of their political and spiritual heritage. We want democracy to survive for all generations to come, not to become the insolvent phantom of tomorrow.

Down the long lane of the history yet to be written, America knows that this world of ours, ever growing smaller, must avoid becoming a community of dreadful fear and hate, and be, instead, a proud confederation of mutual trust and respect.

Such a confederation must be one of equals. The weakest must come to the conference table with the same confidence as do we, protected as we are by our moral, economic, and military strength. That table, though scarred by many past frustrations, cannot be abandoned for the certain agony of the battlefield.

Disarmament, with mutual honor and confidence, is a continuing imperative. Together we must learn how to compose differences, not with arms, but with intellect and decent purpose. Because this need is so sharp and apparent, I confess that I lay down my official responsibilities in this field with a definite sense of disappointment. As one who has witnessed the horror and the lingering sadness of war - as one who knows that another war could utterly destroy this civilization which has been so slowly and painfully built over thousands of years - I wish I could say tonight that a lasting peace is in sight.

Happily, I can say that war has been avoided. Steady progress toward our ultimate goal has been made. But so much remains to be done. As a private citizen, I shall never cease to do what little I can to help the world advance along that road.

So - in this my last good night to you as your President - I thank you for the many opportunities you have given me for public service in war and peace. I trust that in that service you find some things worthy; as for the rest of it, I know you will find ways to improve performance in the future.

You and I, my fellow citizens, need to be strong in our faith that all nations, under God, will reach the goal of peace with justice. May we be ever unswerving in devotion to principle, confident but humble with power, diligent in pursuit of the Nation's great goals.

To all the peoples of the world, I once more give expression to America's prayerful and continuing aspiration.

We pray that peoples of all faiths, all races, all nations, may have their great human needs satisfied - that those now denied opportunity shall come to enjoy it to the full - that all who yearn for freedom may experience its spiritual blessings - that those who have freedom will understand, also, its heavy responsibilities   that all who are insensitive to the needs of others will learn charity - that the scourges of poverty, disease, and ignorance will be made to disappear from the earth - and that, in the goodness of time, all peoples will come to live together in a peace guaranteed by the binding force of mutual respect and love.

Dwight D. Eisenhower

Afterward
Dwight D. Eisenhower died on March 28, 1969.

Selected Reading

Ambrose, Stephen E., *Eisenhower*, 1984.
_____, *Eisenhower: Soldier and President*, 1990.
Burk, Robert F., *Dwight D. Eisenhower, Hero & Politician*, 1986.
Eisenhower, Dwight, *Crusade In Europe*, 1948.
_____, *Mandate For Change*, 1963.
_____, *Waging Peace*, 1965.
Lee, R. Alton, *Dwight D. Eisenhower, Soldier and Statesman*, 1981.
Lyon, Peter, *Eisenhower: Portrait of the Hero*, 1974.
McCann, Kevin, *America's Man of Destiny: An Intimate Biography of General Eisenhower*, 1952.
Miller, Francis T., *Eisenhower, Man and Soldier*, 1944.
Morin, Relman, *Dwight D. Eisenhower: A Gauge of Greatness*, 1969.
Perret, Geoffrey, *Eisenhower*, 1999.

Betty Friedan
The Power Of Our Sisterhood
August 26, 1970

I propose that on Wednesday, August 26, 1970, we call a twenty four hour general strike, a resistance, both passive and active, of all women in America against the concrete conditions of their oppression.

- Betty Friedan, 1970

Betty (Goldstein) Friedan was born in Peoria, Illinois on February 4, 1921, the daughter of Harry and Miriam (Horwitz) Goldstein. Educated at Smith College, Friedan pursued a writing career. She married and, still writing part-time, began a family. In 1963 Friedan, a stay-at-home suburban mother, published *The Feminine Mystique,* which sold four million copies and started the modern women's movement. Friedan had spent five years interviewing suburban women like herself. She termed them *The Happy Housewives,* and found they shared her own dissatisfaction in living up to the myth of *happy female domesticity. The Feminine Mystique* argued that American society had formed a new and harmful fantasy - *A Woman's Place Is In The Home* - that dictated to women that fulfillment could only be found in marriage and motherhood.

The National Organization for Women, led by Betty Friedan, was founded in 1966. NOW members were dismissed and scorned as *Women's Libbers.* In early 1970 Friedan proposed that, on the fiftieth anniversary of the Women's Suffrage Amendment, NOW stage a nationwide event that could not be dismissed - a Women's Strike Day. NOW staged Strike Day rallies in ninety cities. In New York City, the Statute of Liberty was draped with the banner - *Women Of The World Unite!* - and there was a mile-long march down Fifth Avenue which drew tens of thousands.

On August 26, 1970, Women's Strike Day, in New York City's Bryant Park, Betty Friedan delivered this landmark speech, *The Power Of Our Sisterhood.*

After tonight, the politics of this nation will never be the same. By our numbers here tonight, by women who marched curb-to-curb down Fifth Avenue - women who had never marched before in their own cause, with veterans of the first battle of the vote, with young high school students, black women with white women, housewives with women who work in factories and offices, women whose husbands are rich and who discovered that all women are poor - we learned. We learned what none of us had dared to hope - the power of our solidarity, the power of our sisterhood. We learned that we have the power to change the conditions that oppress us. We learned that we have the power to restructure the social institutions that today are so completely man's world. We learned who the enemy was, and I say *was*, because by the very act of learning this, by our actions tonight, that enemy went away. We faced the enemy and the enemy was us, was our own lack of self-confidence, was woman's self-denigration. We know now, if we didn't know before, that the enemy is not man. Many men joined us in this march, men who are part of our true sex role revolution, who dare by wearing their hair long to say *No* to that tight-lipped, muscled, obsolete image of masculinity, to say,

No, we don't have to be dominant and superior to everybody in the world to prove our manhood. We can be compassionate. We can be tender. We can be gentle. We can be sensitive. We can admit sometimes we are afraid and we can even cry, and we are men.

These men will welcome their liberation, with ours, from this tyranny of roles as they have been defined by others. And they will welcome women who finally and at last are beginning to spell their own names. We spell our own names here tonight. We spell our names as people first. And the liberation involved here is true sexual liberation.

The sexual liberation from the Playboy bunny image that is just the other side of the repression, of the puritanical obsession that says sex is dirty. We will not only free ourselves, we will free men from the torment that makes it impossible to make love, not war, for when we liberate ourselves from the discrimination and the barriers that keep us from being full people, then men also will be free.

Anthropologists know that in any society that denies women full humanity and full participation in the mainstream, in that society sex is an obsession or a repression, and in that society violence breeds. The violence that is napalming the children in Cambodia is linked to the loneliness, anguish, guilt and hostilities of the war between the sexes that we transcend tonight. In liberating ourselves, we must find our human voice and the strength to unite with our brothers, with the youth, with the blacks, in a common coalition against repression in this country, against fascism, against death and war.

There is nothing inevitable about this or any other revolution. We make it happen ourselves. The meaning of this strike is that we have no more time to waste in navel-gazing rap sessions; we have no more time to waste in sterile dead ends of man hatred, mistaking the rage caused by the conditions that oppress us for a sexual rage that is simply a temporary aberration. This is not a bedroom war. This is a political movement and it will change the politics. We are not a small minority, we who are now fifty-three percent of the people. We have the power to act against the conditions that oppress us and to change them. We will use it. Our strike has just begun. It will not end until we have real equality of opportunity in education and employment, a whole network in this and every city of universal twenty-four-hour child-care centers, and the right, the inalienable human right, to control our own bodies, to medical help in abortion. It will not end until our political movement stops voting for the best of two men and we have fifty women in the Senate.

We serve notice, in our strike here tonight, that any senator who dares to trifle in any way with the Equal Rights Amendment trifles with his political future, for women will not forgive and will not forget. There is no way any man, woman or child can escape the nature of our revolution, of this great movement as it manifests itself here tonight and in other cities where women are marching. What we do here will transform society, though it may not be exactly what Karl Marx or anyone else meant by revolutionary. We are all the Karl Marxes of this revolution. We, the women, must create, existentially, our own ideology, though we have much to learn from others. It will mean a new kind of structuring of professions, of work, of the economy. What will happen to the economy when women are no longer so mired in self-denigration from prenubility to late senility that they can be sold anything and everything in order to catch and keep a man? What will happen to architecture, to city planning, when women are no longer the unpaid free servants of the home?

Part of the unfinished business of our revolution is to put a real economic value on the work women do in the home. All of us are housewives, but from now on it shouldn't be housewives - *housespouses* is a better word. Both of us will share the world inside the home and walk equally in the world outside the home.

And finally, there will be a new kind of creativity, not only a new definition of love, but, as we define ourselves, a new image of woman and of man, and a new theology. The great debate of the 1960's in theology was *Is God Dead?*

The debate of the 1970's will be *Is God He?* I do not say that God should be She, but unless we can see the highest possible creation and creativity in female roles as well as in male, we have not reached the next step of human evolution.

In the joy on every woman's face here tonight, in the sense that all of us have that we are sisters, that all women are beautiful, in our ability to transcend the lines of nation, class, man-made politics, and race that divide us, in our affirmation of ourselves as women, we have felt a transcendent joy tonight. Woman's life has been confined by dailyness - cooking the dinner that gets eaten, and must be cooked again, sweeping the floor that must be swept every day - and transcended only by the biological birth of our children. It has never been completely human because so few of us have had this great experience that all of us have had tonight, of creating history, of taking the torch from those great women who won us the vote fifty years ago and carrying that torch high so that it shines on the lives, not only of our daughters, but on our own selves in self-affirmation.

In the religion of my ancestors, there was a prayer that Jewish men said every morning. They prayed, *Thank thee, Lord, that I was not born a woman.* Today I feel, feel for the first time, feel absolutely sure that all women are going to be able to say, as I say tonight, *Thank thee, Lord, that I was born a woman, for this day.*

Betty Friedan

Afterward

Betty Friedan continues to write and lecture on women's issues.

Selected Reading

Friedan, Betty, *The Feminine Mystique*, 1963.

_____, *It Changed My Life*, 1976.

_____, *The Second Stage*, 1981.

_____, *The Fountain Of Age*, 1993.

_____, *Beyond Gender*, 1997.

_____, *Life So Far*, 2000.

Hennessee, Judith A., *Betty Friedan: Her Life*, 1999.

Horowitz, Daniel, *Betty Friedan and the Making of The Feminine Mystique*, 1998.

Lou Gehrig
The Luckiest Man On The Face Of The Earth
July 4, 1939

I knew that as long as I was following Babe Ruth to the plate I could have stood on my head and no one would have known the difference.
- Lou Gehrig

Living in the shadow of the flamboyant Babe Ruth was the quiet, day-to-day baseball superstar Lou Gehrig. Henry Louis Gehrig was born in New York City on June 19, 1903, the son of Henry and Christina (Fack) Gehrig. In 1921, while attending Columbia University on an athletic scholarship, Gehrig was recruited to play for the New York Yankees. On June 1, 1925, after two years in the minor leagues, Gehrig, twenty-one, was placed in the Yankee line-up.

He appeared in that line-up, known as Murderers Row, in every game for the next fifteen years - 2,130 games. For his consecutive game streak, sportswriters nicknamed him *The Iron Horse.* Gehrig was a baseball superstar - in regular season play, appearing in 2,164 games (1925-39), he compiled a lifetime batting average of .340, including 493 home runs and a fielding average of .991. In post-season play, appearing in 34 World Series games (1926-28, '32, '36-'38), he compiled a batting average of .361, including 10 home runs and a fielding average of .997.

On April 30, 1939, after 2,130 consecutive games, Gehrig, suffering from a mysterious illness that left him weak and uncoordinated, removed himself from the Yankee line-up. On his thirty-sixth birthday, June 19, 1939, Lou Gehrig was diagnosed with ALS, amyotrophic lateral sclerosis, a degenerative neuromuscular disease. It was a death sentence.

On July 4, 1939, in Yankee Stadium before a capacity crowd of 61,808 fans, friends, and teammates, Lou Gehrig, almost too emotional to speak, delivered this courageous landmark speech, *The Luckiest Man On The Face Of The Earth.*

Lou Gehrig

Fans, for the past two weeks you have been reading about a bad break I got. Yet today I consider myself the luckiest man on the face of the earth. I have been in ballparks for seventeen years and I have never received anything but kindness and encouragement from you fans. Look at these grand men. Which of you wouldn't consider it the highlight of his career just to associate with them for even one day? Sure, I'm lucky. Who wouldn't consider it an honor to have known Jacob Ruppert? Also, the builder of baseball's greatest empire, Ed Barrow? To have spent six years with that wonderful little fellow, Miller Huggins? Then to have spent the next nine years with that outstanding leader, that smart student of psychology, the best manager in baseball today, Joe McCarthy? Sure, I'm lucky. When the New York Giants, a team you would give your right arm to beat, and vice versa, sends you a gift, that's something. When everybody down to the groundskeepers and those boys in white coats remember you with trophies, that's something. When you have a father and mother who work all their lives so that you can have an education and build your body, it's a blessing. When you have a wife who has been a tower of strength and shown more courage than you dreamed existed, that's the finest I know. So I close in saying that I might have had a bad break, but I have an awful lot to live for. Thank you.

Afterward
Lou Gehrig died on June 2, 1941.

Selected Reading
Gallico, Paul, *Lou Gehrig: Pride of the Yankees*, 1942.
Robinson, Ray, *Iron Horse: Lou Gehrig in His Time*, 1990.

Movies:
Pride Of The Yankees, 1942.

Barry Goldwater
Extremism In Defense Of Liberty Is No Vice
July 16, 1964

To insist on a strong American military is not war-mongering. It is peace-mongering. — **Barry Goldwater, August 11, 1964**

Barry Morris Goldwater was born in Phoenix, Arizona on January 1, 1909, the son of Baron and Josephine (Williams) Goldwater. Starting out as a clerk in the family-owned department store, Goldwater rose to its presidency, where he served, with a break for service in World War II, until entering politics. A harsh critic of the Roosevelt and Truman Administrations' *liberal agenda*, Goldwater, a Republican, was elected Arizona's U.S. Senator in 1952. Practicing *the politics of plain talk*, Goldwater earned a national reputation as an outspoken conservative. In 1960 he published the best-selling book, *The Conscience of a Conservative*, writing, *The conscience of a conservative opposes all who would debase the freedom of the individual. Freedom requires the establishment of order, but political power is limited and must be kept within its proper bounds.* In 1962, in a second best-selling book, *Why Not Victory?*, Goldwater wrote of the Cold War, *We are dealing with an enemy who is insatiable, whose creed demands slavery for everyone, Americans included. The more we give in to him, the more he is encouraged to demand.*

Senator Goldwater became the leading conservative critic of the liberal policies of the Democratic Party's Kennedy and Johnson Administrations - *I suggest that men committed to collectivism in domestic affairs are ill-equipped, indeed, almost incapable, of combating the disease of worldwide collectivist slavery.* In 1964 Barry Goldwater ran for and won the Republican Party's Presidential nomination.

On July 16, 1964, at the Republican National Convention in San Francisco, Barry Goldwater accepted his Party's Presidential nomination by delivering this landmark speech, *Extremism In Defense Of Liberty Is No Vice.*

I accept your nomination with a deep sense of humility. I accept, too, the responsibility that goes with it, and I seek your continued help and your continued guidance. My fellow Republicans, our cause is too great for any man to feel worthy of it. Our task would be too great for any man did he not have with him the heart and the hands of this great Republican party. And I promise you tonight that every fiber of my being is consecrated to our cause, that nothing shall be lacking from the struggle that can be brought to it by enthusiasm, by devotion, and plain hard work.

In this world no person, no party, can guarantee anything, but what we can do and what we shall do is to deserve victory and victory will be ours. The Good Lord raised this mighty Republic to be a home for the brave and to flourish as the land of the free - not to stagnate in the swampland of collectivism, not to cringe before the bully of Communism.

Now, my fellow Americans, the tide has been running against freedom. Our people have followed false prophets. We must, and we shall, return to proven ways - not because they are old, but because they are true. We must, and we shall, set the tide running again in the cause of freedom. And this party, with its every action, every word, every breath, and every heartbeat, has but a single resolve, and that is freedom.

Freedom made orderly for this nation by our constitutional government. Freedom under a government limited by laws of nature and of nature's God. Freedom balanced so that order lacking liberty will not become the slavery of the prison cell, balanced so that liberty lacking order will not become the license of the mob and of the jungle.

Now, we Americans understand freedom; we have earned it; we have lived for it; and we have died for it. This nation and its people are freedom's models in a searching world. We can be freedom's missionaries in a doubting world. But, ladies and gentlemen, first we must renew freedom's mission in our own hearts and in our own homes.

During four futile years, the Administration which we shall replace has distorted and lost that faith. It has talked and talked and talked and talked the words of freedom, but it has failed and failed and failed in the works of freedom. Now failure cements the wall of shame in Berlin; failures blot the sands of shame at the Bay of Pigs; failures marked the slow death of freedom in Laos; failures infest the jungles of Vietnam; and failures haunt the houses of our once great alliances and undermine the greatest bulwark ever erected by free nations, the NATO community. Failures proclaim lost leadership, obscure purpose, weakening wills, and the risk of inciting our sworn enemies to new aggressions and to new excesses.

And because of this Administration we are tonight a world divided. We are a nation becalmed. We have lost the brisk pace of diversity and the genius of individual creativity. We are plodding along at a pace set by centralized planning, red tape, rules without responsibility, and regimentation with recourse. Rather than useful jobs in our country, people have been offered bureaucratic make-work; rather than moral leadership, they have been given bread and circuses; they have been given spectacles, and yes, they've even been given scandals.

Tonight there is violence in our streets, corruption in our highest offices, aimlessness among our youth, anxiety among our elderly, and there's a virtual despair among the many who look beyond material success toward the inner meaning of their lives. And where examples of morality should be set, the opposite is seen. Small men seeking great wealth or power have too often and too long turned even the highest levels of public service into mere personal opportunity.

Now, certainly simple honesty is not too much to demand of men in government. We find it in most. Republicans demand it from everyone. They demand it from everyone no matter how exalted or protected his position might be.

The growing menace in our country tonight - to personal safety, to life, to limb and property, in homes, in churches, on the playgrounds and places of business, particularly in our great cities - is the mounting concern, or should be, of every thoughtful citizen in the United States. Security from domestic violence, no less than from foreign aggression, is the most elementary and fundamental purpose of any government, and a government that cannot fulfill this purpose is one that cannot long command the loyalty of its citizens.

History shows us, demonstrates, that nothing - nothing - prepares the way for tyranny more than the failure of public officials to keep the streets safe from bullies and marauders. Now we Republicans see all this as more - much more - than the result of mere political differences, or mere political mistakes. We see this as the result of a fundamentally and absolutely wrong view of man, his nature, and his destiny.

Those who seek to live your lives for you, to take your liberty in return for relieving you of yours, those who elevate the state and downgrade the citizen, must see ultimately a world in which earthly power can be substituted for Divine Will. And this nation was founded upon the rejection of that notion and upon the acceptance of God as the author of freedom.

Now those who seek absolute power, even though they seek it to do what they regard as good, are simply demanding the right to enforce their own version of heaven on earth, and let me remind you they are the very ones who always create the most hellish tyranny.

Absolute power does corrupt, and those who seek it must be suspect and must be opposed. Their mistaken course stems from false notions, ladies and gentlemen, of equality. Equality, rightly understood, as our founding fathers understood it, leads to liberty and to the emancipation of creative differences; wrongly understood, as it has been so tragically in our time, it leads first to conformity and then to despotism.

Fellow Republicans, it is the cause of Republicanism to resist concentrations of power, private or public, which enforce such conformity and inflict such despotism. It is the cause of Republicanism to insure that power remains in the hands of the people - and, so help us God, that is exactly what a Republican President will do with the help of a Republican Congress.

It is further the cause of Republicanism to restore a clear understanding of the tyranny of man over man in the world at large. It is our cause to dispel the foggy thinking which avoids hard decisions in the delusion that a world of conflict will somehow resolve itself into a world of harmony, if we just don't rock the boat or irritate the forces of aggression - and this is hogwash.

It is further the cause of Republicanism to remind ourselves, and the world, that only the strong can remain free, that only the strong can keep the peace. Now I needn't remind you, or my fellow Americans regardless of party, that Republicans have shouldered this hard responsibility and marched in this cause before. It was Republican leadership under Dwight Eisenhower that kept the peace, and passed along to this Administration the mightiest arsenal for defense the world has ever known.

And I needn't remind you that it was the strength and the believable will of the Eisenhower years that kept the peace by using our strength, by using it in the Formosa Strait, and in Lebanon, and by showing it courageously at all times. It was during those Republican years that the thrust of Communist imperialism was blunted. It was during those years of Republican leadership that this world moved closer not to war but closer to peace than at any other time in the last three decades.

And I needn't remind you, but I will, that it's been during Democratic years that our strength to deter war has been stilled and even gone into a planned decline. It has been during Democratic years that we have weakly stumbled into conflicts, timidly refusing to draw our own lines against aggression, deceitfully refusing to tell even our own people of our full participation and tragically letting our finest men die on battlefields unmarked by purpose, unmarked by pride or the prospect of victory. Yesterday it was Korea; tonight it is Vietnam. Make no bones of this. Don't try to sweep this under the rug. We are at war in Vietnam. And yet the President, who is the Commander-in-Chief of our forces, refuses to say - refuses to say, mind you - whether or not the objective over there is victory, and his Secretary of Defense continues to mislead and misinform the American people, and enough of it has gone by.

And I needn't remind you, but I will - it has been during Democratic years that a billion persons were cast into Communist captivity and their fate cynically sealed. Today in our beloved country we have an Administration which seems eager to deal with Communism in every coin known - from gold to wheat, from consulates to confidence, and even human freedom itself.

Now the Republican cause demands that we brand Communism as the principal disturber of peace in the world today. Indeed, we should brand it as the only significant disturber of the peace. And we must make clear that until its goals of conquest are absolutely renounced, and its relations with all nations tempered, Communism and the governments it now controls are enemies of every man on earth who is or wants to be free.

Now, we here in America can keep the peace only if we remain vigilant and only if we remain strong. Only if we keep our eyes open and keep our guard up can we prevent war.

And I want to make this abundantly clear - I don't intend to let peace or freedom be torn from our grasp because of lack of strength, or lack of will - and that I promise you Americans. I believe that we must look beyond the defense of freedom today to its extension tomorrow. I believe that the Communism which boasts it will bury us will instead give way to the forces of freedom. And I can see in the distant and yet recognizable future the outlines of a world worthy of our dedication, our every risk, our every effort, our every sacrifice along the way. Yes, a world that will redeem the suffering of those who will be liberated from tyranny.

I can see, and I suggest that all thoughtful men must contemplate, the flowering of an Atlantic civilization, the whole world of Europe reunified and free, trading openly across its borders, communicating openly across the world. This is a goal far, far more meaningful than a moon shot. It's a truly inspiring goal for all free men to set for themselves during the latter half of the twentieth century. I can see, and all free men must thrill to, the events of this Atlantic civilization joined by a straight ocean highway to the United States. What a destiny! What a destiny can be ours to stand as a great central pillar linking Europe, the Americas, and the venerable and vital peoples and cultures of the Pacific.

I can see a day when all the Americas - North and South - will be linked in a mighty system, a system in which the errors and misunderstandings of the past will be submerged one by one in a rising tide of prosperity and interdependence. We know that the misunderstandings of centuries are not to be wiped away in a day or wiped away in an hour. But we pledge that human sympathy - what our neighbors to the South call an attitude of simpatico - no less than enlightened self-interest will be our guide.

And I can see this Atlantic civilization galvanizing and guiding emergent nations everywhere. Now I know this freedom is not the fruit of every soil. I know that our own freedom was achieved through centuries by unremitting efforts by brave and wise men. And I know that the road to freedom is a long and a challenging road, and I know also that some men may walk away from it, that some men resist challenge, accepting the false security of governmental paternalism.

And I pledge that the America I envision in the years ahead will extend its hand in help in teaching and in cultivation so that all new nations will be at least encouraged to go our way, so that they will not wander down the dark alleys of tyranny or to the dead-end streets of collectivism.

My fellow Republicans, we do no man a service by hiding freedom's light under a bushel of mistaken humility.

I seek an America proud of its past, proud of its ways, proud of its dreams, and determined actively to proclaim them. But our examples to the world must, like charity, begin at home.

In our vision of a good and decent future, free and peaceful, there must be room, room for the liberation of the energy and the talent of the individual; otherwise our vision is blind at the outset.

We must assure a society here which, while never abandoning the needy, or forsaking the helpless, nurtures incentives and opportunity for the creative and the productive.

We must know the whole good is the product of many single contributions. And I cherish the day when our children once again will restore as heroes the sort of men and women who, unafraid and undaunted, pursue the truth, strive to cure disease, subdue and make fruitful our natural environment, and produce the inventive engines of production, science, and technology.

This nation, whose creative people have enhanced this entire span of history, should again thrive upon the greatness of all those things which we - we as individual citizens - can and should do.

During Republican years, this again will be a nation of men and women, of families proud of their role, jealous of their responsibilities, unlimited in their aspirations - a nation where all who can will be self-reliant.

We Republicans see in our constitutional form of government the great framework which assures the orderly but dynamic fulfillment of the whole man, and we see the whole man as the great reason for instituting orderly government in the first place.

We can see in private property, and in economy based upon and fostering private property, the one way to make government a durable ally of the whole man rather than his determined enemy. We see in the sanctity of private property the only durable foundation for constitutional government in a free society.

And beyond that we see and cherish diversity of ways, diversity of thoughts, of motives, and accomplishments. We don't seek to live anyone's life for him. We only seek to secure his rights, guarantee him opportunity to strive, with government performing only those needed and constitutionally sanctioned tasks which cannot otherwise be performed.

We Republicans seek a government that attends to its inherent responsibilities of maintaining a stable monetary and fiscal climate, encouraging a free and a competitive economy, and enforcing law and order. Thus do we seek inventiveness, diversity, and creative difference within a stable order, for we Republicans define government's role where needed at many, many levels, preferably though the one closest to the people involved - our towns and our cities, then our counties, then our states, then our regional contacts, and only then the national government.

That, let me remind you, is the land of liberty built by decentralized power. On it also we must have balance between the branches of government at every level. Balance, diversity, creative difference - these are the elements of Republican equation. Republicans agree heartily to disagree on many, many of their applications. But we have never disagreed on the basic fundamental issues of why you and I are Republicans.

This is a party - this Republican party is a party for free men - not for blind followers and not for conformists. Back in 1858 Abraham Lincoln said this of the Republican party, and I quote him because he probably could have said it during the last week or so, *It was composed of strained, discordant, and even hostile elements.* Yet all of these elements agreed on one paramount objective - to arrest the progress of slavery, and place it in the course of ultimate extinction.

Today, as then, but more urgently and more broadly than then, the task of preserving and enlarging freedom at home and of safeguarding it from the forces of tyranny abroad is great enough to challenge all our resources and to require all our strength. Anyone who joins us in all sincerity we welcome. Those who do not care for our cause, we don't expect to enter our ranks in any case. And let our Republicanism so focused and so dedicated not be made fuzzy and futile by unthinking and stupid labels.

I would remind you that extremism in the defense of liberty is no vice. And let me remind you also that moderation in the pursuit of justice is no virtue!

By the beauty of the very system, we Republicans are pledged to restore and revitalize; the beauty of this Federal system of ours is in its reconciliation of diversity with unity. We must not see malice in honest differences of opinion, and no matter how great, so long as they are not inconsistent with the pledges we have given to each other in and through our Constitution.

Our Republican cause is not to level out the world or make its people conform in computer-regimented sameness. Our Republican cause is to free our people and light the way for liberty throughout the world. Ours is a very human cause for very humane goals. This party, its good people, and its unquestionable devotion to freedom, will not fulfill the purposes of this campaign which we launch here now until our cause has won the day, inspired the world, and shown the way to a tomorrow worthy of all our yesteryears.

I repeat, I accept your nomination with humbleness, with pride, and you and I are going to fight for the goodness of our land.

Afterward
Barry Goldwater lost the Presidential election of 1964. Richard Nixon later wrote, *If Goldwater ever had a chance to win the Presidency, he lost it that night with that speech.* Goldwater replied to his critics, *I think it was the best speech I every made.*

Barry Goldwater died on May 29, 1998.

Selected Reading
Bell, Jack, *Mr. Conservative: Barry Goldwater,* 1962.
Cook, Fred J., *Barry Goldwater: Extremist of the Right,* 1964.
Goldberg, Robert A., *Barry Goldwater,* 1995.
Goldwater, Barry M., *With No Apologies: The Personal and Political Memoirs of United States Senator Barry M. Goldwater,* 1979.
Goldwater, Barry M., with Jack Casserly, *Goldwater,* 1988.

Lyndon Johnson
The Tonkin Gulf
August 4, 1965

*We are not going to send American boys to Southeast Asia to do
what Asian boys ought to be doing for themselves.*
- President Lyndon Johnson, October 21, 1964

The Constitution declares that *The Congress shall have power to
declare war* and *The President shall be Commander-in-Chief of the
Army and Navy of the United States.* In the twentieth century,
the First and Second World Wars were declared by the U.S.
Congress, and the Korean and Vietnam Wars were waged,
without the required Constitutional approval, by U.S. Presi-
dents.

Lyndon Baines Johnson was born on August 27, 1908 near
Stonewall, Texas, the son of Sam and Rebeka Johnson. After serving as a Texas Congressman (1938-47), and a Senator (1948-60), Lyndon Johnson was elected and served as
Vice President (1961-63), and, after the Kennedy Assassination, became President. In the early 1960's the U.S. had
committed 23,000 non-combat *military advisors* to aid South
Vietnam in its war with North Vietnam.

On August 4, 1964, two U.S. warships on patrol in the Gulf
of Tonkin, off the coast of Vietnam, reported that they
had been attacked by North Vietnamese gunboats. President Johnson immediately prepared for Congress The
Tonkin Gulf Resolution - *Congress approves and supports the
determination of the President of the United States, as Commander-
in-Chief, to take all necessary measures to repel any armed attack
against the forces of the United States and to prevent further aggression.*

On August 4, 1965, President Lyndon Johnson addressed
the nation, telling them American forces had been attacked
and that he would ask the Congress for the authority to
retaliate, with this landmark speech, *The Tonkin Gulf.*

57

My fellow Americans, as President and Commander-in-Chief, it is my duty to the American people to report that hostile actions against United States ships on the high seas in the Gulf of Tonkin have today required me to order the military forces of the United States to take action in reply.

The initial attack on the destroyer *Maddox,* on August 2, was repeated today by a number of hostile [North Vietnamese] vessels attacking two U.S. destroyers with torpedoes. The destroyers and supporting aircraft acted at once on the orders I gave after the initial act of aggression. We believe at least two of the attacking boats were sunk. There were no U.S. losses.

The performance of commanders and crews in this engagement is in the highest tradition of the United States Navy. But repeated acts of violence against the Armed Forces of the United States must be met not only with alert defense, but with positive reply. That reply is being given as I speak to you tonight. Air action is now in execution against gunboats and certain supporting facilities in North Vietnam which have been used in these hostile operations.

In the larger sense this new act of aggression, aimed directly at our own forces, again brings home to all of us in the United States the importance of the struggle for peace and security in southeast Asia. Aggression by terror against the peaceful villagers of South Vietnam has now been joined by open aggression on the high seas against the United States of America.

The determination of all Americans to carry out our full commitment to the people and to the government of South Vietnam will be redoubled by this outrage. Yet our response, for the present, will be limited and fitting. We

Americans know, although others appear to forget, the risks of spreading conflict. We still seek no wider war.

. . . . I shall immediately request the Congress to pass a resolution making it clear that our Government is united in its determination to take all necessary measures in support of freedom and in defense of peace in southeast Asia.

. . . . It is a solemn responsibility to have to order even limited military action by forces whose overall strength is as vast and as awesome as those of the United States of America, but it is my considered conviction, shared throughout your Government, that firmness in the right is indispensable today for peace - that firmness will always be measured. Its mission is peace.

Afterward

On August 6, 1965, Congress passed the Tonkin Gulf Resolution. Under the limited authority of the Resolution, Lyndon Johnson ordered, on February 7, 1965, the bombing of North Vietnam and, on July 28, 1965, committed the first 100,000 of an eventual 500,000 combat troops. On March 31, 1968, Lyndon Johnson admitted his own personal defeat and told the nation, *I shall not seek, and I will not accept, the nomination of my party for another term as your President.*

Lyndon Johnson died on January 22, 1973.

Selected Reading

Berman, Larry, *Lyndon Johnson's War*, 1989.
Gardner, Lloyd C., *Pay Any Price*, 1995.
Goulden, Joseph, *Truth Is The First Casualty: The Tonkin Gulf Affair*, 1969.
Moise, Edwin E., *Tonkin Gulf and the Escalation of the Vietnam War*, 1996.
Windchy, Eugene G., *Tonkin Gulf*, 1971.

Mother Jones
The Wail Of The Children
July 28, 1903

I pray for the dead and fight like hell for the living!
- **Mother Jones**

Mary Harris Jones, called by President Theodore Roosevelt *the most dangerous woman in America*, was born on August 1, 1837 in Cork, Ireland, the child of Richard and Ellen (Cotter) Jones. Immigrating to America, Jones joined the Knights of Labor, an industrial workers union, and gained fame as a union organizer and speaker at labor rallies. She agitated for an eight-hour day - *The workers ask only for bread and a shortening of the long hours of toil.* - and an end to child labor - *All day long, all night long, tiny babies of six-year-olds with the faces of sixty-year-olds did an eight-hour shift for ten cents a day.* Working with the Knights, the American Railway Union, and the United Mine Workers, the woman called *Mother* by the workers, Jones traveled the country, urging underpaid, over-worked laborers to *fight the good fight against wrong.*

In the early 1900's there were an estimated two million children, ranging in age from five to sixteen, working in American factories. On May 29, 1903, Philadelphia's textile workers, including an estimated five thousand child workers, went on strike, demanding a reduction in their workweek from sixty to fifty-five hours. On July 7 Mother Jones, to publicize the plight of these child workers, organized a 125-mile Children's March from Philadelphia - *where mansions were built on the broken bones of children* - through New York City - *where we will parade up and down Wall Street to show the millionaires the little emaciated boys who have earned their millions for them* - to Oyster Bay, New York, the summer home of President Theodore Roosevelt.

On July 28, 1903, the Children's March arrived in New York City, where Mother Jones delivered this landmark speech, *The Wail Of the Children.*

After a long and weary march, with more miles to travel, we are on our way to see President Roosevelt at Oyster Bay. We will ask him to recommend the passage of a bill by Congress to protect children against the greed of the manufacturer. We want him to hear the wail of the children, who never have a chance to go to school, but work from ten to eleven hours a day in the textile mills of Philadelphia, weaving the carpets that he and you walk on, and the curtains and clothes of the people.

Fifty years ago there was a cry against slavery, and the men of the North gave up their lives to stop the selling of black children on the block. Today the white child is sold for $2 a week, and even by his parents, to the manufacturer. Fifty years ago the black babies were sold C.O.D. Today the white baby is sold to the manufacturer on the installment plan. He might die at his tasks and the manufacturer with the automobile and the yacht and the daughter who talks French to a poodle dog, as you can see any day at Twenty-third Street and Broadway when they roll by, could not afford to pay $2 a week for the child that might die, except on the present installment plan. What the President can do is to recommend a measure and send a message to Congress which will break the chains of the white children slaves. . . . We will ask in the name of the aching hearts of these little ones that they be emancipated. I will tell the President that I saw men in Madison Square last night sleeping on the benches and that the country can have no greatness while one unfortunate lies out at night without a bed to sleep on. I will tell him that the prosperity he boasts of is the prosperity of the rich wrung from the poor.

In Georgia where children work day and night in the cotton mills they have just passed a bill to protect song birds. What about the little children from whom all song is gone?

The trouble is that the fellers in Washington don't care. . . . When labor cries for aid for the little ones they turn their backs and will not listen. . . . I asked a man in prison once how he happened to get there. He had stolen a pair of shoes. I told him that if he had stolen a railroad he could be a United States Senator. One hour of justice is worth an age of praying.

You are told that every American-born male citizen has a chance of being President. I tell you that the hungry man without a bed in the park would sell his chance for a good square meal, and these little toilers, deformed, dwarfed in body, soul, and morality, with nothing but toil before them and no chance for schooling, don't even have the dream that they might some day have a chance at the Presidential chair.

They are trying to teach monkeys in the cages to talk. The monkeys are too wise, for they fear that then the manufacturers might buy them for slaves in their factories. In 1860 the workingmen had the advantage in the percentage of the country's wealth. Today statistics at Washington show that with billions of wealth the wage earners' share is but 10 percent. We are going to tell the President of these things.

Afterward
Mother Jones wrote to President Roosevelt, *The child of today is the man or woman of tomorrow. I have with me children who have walked one hundred miles. I will bring them before you at any time you may set.* Roosevelt refused.

Mother Jones died on November 30, 1930.

Selected Reading
Jones, Mary Harris, *The Autobiography of Mother Jones*, 1925.
Josephson, Judith, *Mother Jones*, 1997.

Barbara Jordan
Watergate
July 25, 1974

I have decided to vote for impeachment, and I'm going to say why.
- Barbara Jordan, July 25, 1974

The Chair recognizes the Congresswoman from Texas, Ms. Jordan. On July 25, 1974, during the nationally televised Watergate impeachment hearings, it came the turn of Barbara Jordan, one of the few African American women in the House of Representatives, to render her decision on the impeachment of President Richard Nixon.

Barbara Charline Jordan was born on February 21, 1936 in Houston, Texas, the child of Benjamin and Arlyen (Patten) Jordan. Educated at Texas Southern University and Boston University Law School, Barbara Jordan served two terms in the Texas Senate before her 1972 election to the U.S. House of Representatives.

Watergate was a conspiracy to commit and cover up crimes by the Nixon White House directed against their *enemies.* After hearing testimony on President Nixon's knowledge of the crimes - *What did the President know and when did he know it?* - and his unsuccessful attempts at a cover-up (The Saturday Night Massacre, The 18-½ Minute Gap, The *Smoking Gun* Tape), the House Judiciary Committee drew up Articles of Impeachment. Under the Constitution, a President can only be removed from office for *high crimes and misdemeanors.* Barbara Jordan, a member of the House Judiciary Committee, wrote, *Failure to take care, to see that the laws are faithfully executed . . . that couldn't be an impeachable offense, could it? That couldn't fall under the high crimes and misdemeanors, could it?*

On July 25, 1974, after listening to testimony and examining the evidence, Barbara Jordan explained her decision to vote for impeachment in this landmark speech, *Watergate.*

Earlier today we heard the beginning of the Preamble to the Constitution of the United States, *We, the people.* It is a very eloquent beginning. But when that document was completed on the 17th of September in 1787, I was not included in that *We, the people.* I felt somehow for many years that George Washington and Alexander Hamilton just left me out by mistake. But through the process of amendment, interpretation, and court decision I have finally been included in *We, the people.*

Today, I am an inquisitor. I believe hyperbole would not be fictional and would not overstate the solemness that I feel right now. My faith in the Constitution is whole, it is complete, it is total. I am not going to sit here and be an idle spectator to the diminution, the subversion, the destruction of the Constitution.

Who can so properly be the inquisitors for the nation as the representatives of the nation themselves? [The Federalist Papers No. 65] The subject of its jurisdiction are those offenses which proceed from the misconduct of public men. That is what we are talking about. In other words, the jurisdiction comes from the abuse of violation of some public trust. It is wrong, I suggest, it is a misreading of the Constitution for any member here to assert that for a member to vote for an Article of Impeachment means that that member must be convinced that the President should be removed from office. The Constitution doesn't say that. The powers relating to impeachment are an essential check in the hands of this body, the legislature, against and upon the encroachment of the Executive.

In establishing the division between the two branches of the legislature, the House and the Senate, assigning to the one the right to accuse and to the other the right to judge, the Framers of this Constitution were very astute. They did not make the accusers and the judges the same person.

We know the nature of impeachment. We have been talking about it awhile now. *It is chiefly designed for the President and his high ministers* to somehow be called into account. It is designed to *bridle* the Executive if he engages in excesses. *It is designed as a method of national inquest into the conduct of public men.* [The Federalist Papers No. 65] The Framers confined in the Congress the power, if need be, to remove the President in order to strike a delicate balance between a President swollen with power and grown tyrannical, and preservation of the independence of the Executive. The nature of impeachment is a narrowly channeled exception to the separation of powers maxim - the Federal Convention of 1787 said that. It limited impeachment to high crimes and misdemeanors and discounted and opposed the term *maladministration. It is to be used only for great misdemeanors*, so it was said in the North Carolina Ratification Convention. And in the Virginia Ratification Convention, *We do not trust our liberty to a particular branch. We need one branch to check the others.*

The North Carolina Ratification Convention - *No one need be afraid that officers who commit oppression will pass with immunity.*

Prosecutions of impeachments will seldom fail to agitate the passions of the whole community, said Hamilton in the Federalist Papers No. 65. *And to divide it into parties more or less friendly or inimical to the accused.*

I do not mean political parties in that sense.

The drawing of political lines goes to the motivation behind impeachment; but impeachment must proceed within the confines of the constitutional term, *high crime and misdemeanors.*

Of the impeachment process, it was Woodrow Wilson who said that, *Nothing short of the grossest offenses against the plain law of the land will suffice to give them speed and effectiveness. Indignation so great as to overgrow party interest may secure a conviction; but nothing else can.*

Commonsense would be revolted if we engaged upon this process for petty reasons. Congress has a lot to do. Appropriations, tax reform, health insurance, campaign finance reform, housing, environmental protection, energy sufficiency, mass transportation. Pettiness cannot be allowed to stand in the face of such overwhelming problems. So today we are not being petty. We are trying to be big because the task we have before us is a big one.

This morning in a discussion of the evidence we were told that the evidence which purports to support the allegations of misuse of the CIA by the President is thin. We are told that that evidence is insufficient. What that recital of the evidence this morning did not include is what the President did know on June 23, 1972. The President did know that it was Republican money, that it was money from the Committee for the Re-Election of the President, which was found in the possession of one of the burglars arrested on June 17.

What the President did know on June 23 was the prior activities of E. Howard Hunt, which included his participation in the break-in of Daniel Ellsberg's psychiatrist, which included Howard Hunt's participation in the Dita Beard ITT affair, which included Howard Hunt's fabrication of cables designed to discredit the Kennedy administration.

We were further cautioned today that perhaps these proceedings ought to be delayed because certainly there would be new evidence forthcoming from the President of the

United States. There has not oven been an obfuscated indication that this committee would receive any additional materials from the President. The committee subpoena is outstanding and if the President wants to supply that material, the committee sits here.

The fact is that yesterday, the American people waited with great anxiety for 8 hours, not knowing whether their President would obey an order of the Supreme Court of the United States.

At this point I would like to juxtapose a few of the impeachment criteria with some of the President's actions.

Impeachment criteria - James Madison, from the Virginia Ratification Convention - *If the President be connected in any suspicious manner with any person and there be grounds to believe that he will shelter him, he may be impeached.*

We have heard time and time again that the evidence reflects payment to the defendants of money. The President had knowledge that these funds were being paid and that these were funds collected for the 1972 Presidential campaign.

We know that the President met with Mr. Henry Petersen 27 times to discuss matters related to Watergate and immediately thereafter met with the very persons who were implicated in the information Mr. Petersen was receiving and transmitting to the President. The words are, *If the President be connected in any suspicious manner with any person and there be grounds to believe that he will shelter that person, he may be impeached.*

Justice Story - *Impeachment is intended for occasional and extraordinary cases where a superior power acting for the whole people is put into operation to protect their rights and rescue their liberties from violations.*

. . . . We know about the break-in of the psychiatrist's office. We know that there was absolute complete direction in August 1971 when the President instructed Ehrlichman to *do whatever is necessary.* This instruction led to a surreptitious entry into Dr. Fielding's office.

Protect their rights.

Rescue their liberties from violation.

The South Carolina Ratification Convention impeachment criteria - Those are impeachable *who behave amiss or betray their public trust.*

Beginning shortly after the Watergate break-in and continuing to the present time, the President has engaged in a series of public statements and actions designed to thwart the lawful investigation by Government prosecutors. Moreover, the President has made public announcements and assertions bearing on the Watergate case which the evidence will show he knew to be false.

These assertions, false assertions, impeachable, those who misbehave. Those who *behave amiss or betray their public trust.*

James Madison again at the Constitutional Convention - *A President is impeachable if he attempts to subvert the Constitution.*

The Constitution charges the President with the task of taking care that the laws be faithfully executed, and yet the President has counseled his aides to commit perjury, willfully disregarded the secrecy of grand jury proceedings, concealed surreptitious entry, attempted to compromise a Federal judge while publicly displaying his cooperation with the processes of criminal justice.

Barbara Jordan

A President is impeachable if he attempts to subvert the Constitution.

If the impeachment provision in the Constitution of the United States will not reach the offenses charged here, then perhaps that 18th century Constitution should be abandoned to a 20th century paper shredder. Has the President committed offenses and planned and directed and acquiesced in a course of conduct which the Constitution will not tolerate? That is the question. We know that. We know the question. We should now forthwith proceed to answer the question. It is reason, and not passion, which must guide our deliberations, guide our debate, and guide our decision.

Afterward

On July 27, 1974, the House Judiciary Committee voted to recommend the impeachment of the President. On August 8, 1974, before the House could vote on his impeachment, Richard Nixon resigned his office. On September 8, 1974, his successor, President Gerald Ford, granted him a full pardon.

Barbara Jordan died on January 17, 1996.

Selected Reading

Blue, Rose, and Corinne Naden, *Barbara Jordan*, 1992.
Bryant, Ira B., *Barbara Charline Jordan: From the Ghetto to the Capitol*, 1977.
Haskins, James, *Barbara Jordan*, 1977.
Jordan, Barbara, *Barbara Jordan: A Self-Portrait*, 1979.
Kelin, Norman, and Sabra-Anne Kelin, *Barbara Jordan*, 1993.
Roger, Mary Beth, *Barbara Jordan: American Hero*, 1998.

Helen Keller
The Social Causes Of Blindness
February 14, 1911

I will always - as long as I have breath - work for the handicapped.
-Helen Keller, *The New York Times,* 1960

Helen Keller was born on June 27, 1880 in Tuscumbia, Alabama, the child of Arthur and Kate (Adams) Keller. At nineteen months of age, in February 1881, an undiagnosed illness left Helen blind, deaf, and mute. Keller later wrote, *My eyes and ears were closed and I was plunged into the unconsciousness of a newborn baby.* In 1886 Helen's mother, searching for a way to communicate with her *deaf, dumb, and blind* daughter, hired a specially trained teacher of the deaf - Annie Sullivan. Partially blind herself, Sullivan used a *touch and spell* method, placing Helen Keller's hand into water, and spelling out W-A-T-E-R in finger language - *Suddenly I felt a misty consciousness as of something forgotten - a thrill of returning thought; and somehow the mystery of language was revealed to me.* Helen Keller and Annie Sullivan began a lifelong companionship that lasted fifty years.

An article by Dr. Alexander Graham Bell in praise of Keller's ability to speak via finger language appeared in *The Nation* and made Helen a national celebrity. After learning Braille (and also the rudiments of French, Latin, and Greek), she commenced her formal education, graduating from a School for the Deaf in 1894, The Cambridge School for Young Ladies in 1897, and Radcliffe in 1904.

An activist through her work with the American Federation for the Blind, Helen Keller spent her life traveling the world speaking, through Annie Sullivan, on behalf of both the physically and socially handicapped.

On February 14, 1911, in Boston before the Massachusetts Association for the Blind, Helen Keller delivered this landmark speech, *The Social Causes of Blindness.*

I rejoice that the greatest of all work for the blind, the saving of eyesight, has been laid so clearly before the public. The reports of progress in the conservation of eyes, of health, of life, of all things precious to men are as a trumpet blast summoning us to still greater effort. The devotion of physicians and laymen, and the terrible needs of our fellowmen ought to hearten us in the fight against conquerable misery.

Our worst foes are ignorance, poverty and the unconscious cruelty of our commercial society. These are the causes of much blindness, these are the enemies which destroy the sight of little children and workmen, and undermine the health of mankind. So long as these enemies remain unvanquished, so long will there be blind and crippled men and women.

To study the diseases and accidents by which sight is lost, and to learn how the surgeon can prevent or alleviate them, is not enough. We must strive to put an end to the conditions which cause the disease and accidents.

This case of blindness, the physician says, resulted from ophthalmia. It was really caused by a dark, overcrowded room, by the indecent herding together of human beings in insanitary tenements. We are told that another case was produced by the bursting of a wheel. The real cause was an employer's failure to safeguard his machines. Investigation shows that there are many clever safeguards for machinery which ought to be used in factories, but which are not adopted because their adoption would diminish the employer's profits.

Labor reports indicated that we Americans have been slow, dishonorably slow, in taking measures for the protection of our workmen.

Does it occur to you that the white lace which we wear is darkened by the failing eyes of the lace maker? The trouble is that we do not understand the essential relation between poverty and disease. I do not believe that there is anyone in this city of kind hearts who would willingly receive dividends if he knew that they were paid in part with blinded eyes and broken backs. If you doubt that there is such a connection between our prosperity and the sorrows of the poor, consult those bare but illuminated reports of industrial commissions and labor bureaus. They are less eloquent than oratory. In them you will find the fundamental causes of much blindness and crookedness, of shrunken limbs and degraded minds. These causes must be searched out, and every condition in which blindness breeds must be exposed and abolished. Let our battle cry be, *No preventable disease, no unnecessary poverty, no blinding ignorance among mankind.*

Afterward

In 1957 the fictionalized account of Helen Keller's early life, *The Miracle Worker*, was produced on television. In 1962 it was made into an Academy Award-winning movie. In 1964 Helen Keller was awarded the Presidential Medal of Freedom.

Helen Keller died on June 1, 1968.

Selected Reading

Gibson, William, *The Miracle Worker: A Play*, 1957.
Harrity, Richard, *The Three Lives of Helen Keller*, 1962.
Herrmann, Dorothy, *Helen Keller: A Life*, 1998.
Keller, Helen, *The World I Live In*, 1908.
_____, *Out of the Dark*, 1913.
_____, *The Story of My Life*, 1976.
Lash, Joseph, *Helen and Teacher: The Story of Helen Keller and Anne Sullivan Macy*, 1980.

John F. Kennedy
Ask Not What Your Country Can Do For You
January 20, 1961

A man does what he must - in spite of personal consequences, in spite of obstacles and dangers and pressures - and that is the basis of all human morality.

- John F. Kennedy, *Profiles In Courage,* **1956**

In the election of 1928, the Democratic Party's Presidential candidate, Al Smith, the first Catholic ever to be nominated by a major party for the Presidency, was so badly defeated at the polls that it would be another thirty-two years before any other Catholic would be nominated again.

John Fitzgerald Kennedy was born on May 29, 1917 in Brookline, Massachusetts, the child of Joseph and Rose (Fitzgerald) Kennedy. Educated at Harvard, John Kennedy served in the U.S. Navy during World War Two, earning distinction as the captain of the ill-fated *PT-109.* Kennedy was elected to the House of Representatives from Massachusetts in 1946, and was re-elected in 1948 and 1950. In 1952 he was elected to the Senate from Massachusetts and was re-elected in 1958. In 1960 Kennedy, a Catholic, ran for President. Confronting the *Catholic issue* head on, Kennedy said, *I am not the Catholic candidate for President; I am a candidate for President who happens also to be a Catholic.*

On July 14, 1960, the Democratic National Convention nominated John F. Kennedy as their Presidential candidate. Kennedy spoke of a New Frontier - *The New Frontier of which I speak is not a set of promises - it is a set of challenges. It sums up not what I intend to offer the American people, but to ask of them.* In the election of 1960, John Kennedy defeated Vice President Richard Nixon by just over 100,000 votes.

On January 20, 1961, in Washington, D.C., John F. Kennedy delivered this landmark Inaugural Address, *Ask Not What Your Country Can Do For You.*

We observe today not a victory of party but a celebration of freedom, symbolizing an end as well as a beginning, signifying renewal as well as change. For I have sworn before you and Almighty God the same solemn oath our forebears prescribed nearly a century and three quarters ago.

The world is very different now, for man holds in his mortal hands the power to abolish all forms of human poverty and all forms of human life. And yet the same revolutionary beliefs for which our forebears fought are still at issue around the globe - the belief that the rights of man come not from the generosity of the state but from the hand of God.

We dare not forget today that we are the heirs of that first revolution. Let the word go forth from this time and place, to friend and foe alike, that the torch has been passed to a new generation of Americans, born in this century, tempered by war, disciplined by a hard and bitter peace, proud of our ancient heritage, and unwilling to witness or permit the slow undoing of those human rights to which this nation has always been committed, and to which we are committed today at home and around the world.

Let every nation know, whether it wishes us well or ill, that we shall pay any price, bear any burden, meet any hardship, support any friend, oppose any foe to assure the survival and the success of liberty.

This much we pledge - and more.

To those old allies whose cultural and spiritual origins we share, we pledge the loyalty of faithful friends. United, there is little we cannot do in a host of cooperative ventures. Divided, there is little we can do, for we dare not meet a powerful challenge at odds and split asunder.

To those new states whom we welcome to the ranks of the free, we pledge our word that one form of colonial control shall not have passed away merely to be replaced by a far more iron tyranny. We shall not always expect to find them supporting our view. But we shall always hope to find them strongly supporting their own freedom - and to remember that, in the past, those who foolishly sought power by riding the back of the tiger ended up inside.

To those peoples in the huts and villages of half the globe struggling to break the bonds of mass misery, we pledge our best efforts to help them help themselves, for whatever period is required - not because the Communists may be doing it, not because we seek their votes, but because it is right. If a free society cannot help the many who are poor, it cannot save the few who are rich.

To our sister republics south of our border, we offer a special pledge - to convert our good words into good deeds - in a new alliance for progress - to assist free men and free governments in casting off the chains of poverty. But this peaceful revolution of hope cannot become the prey of hostile powers. Let all our neighbors know that we shall join with them to oppose aggression or subversion anywhere in the Americas. And let every other power know that this Hemisphere intends to remain the master of its own house.

To that world assembly of sovereign states, the United Nations, our last best hope in an age where the instruments of war have far outpaced the instruments of peace, we renew our pledge of support, to prevent it from becoming merely a forum for invective, to strengthen its shield of the new and the weak - and to enlarge the area in which its writ may run.

Finally, to those nations who would make themselves our adversary, we offer not a pledge but a request - that both sides begin anew the quest for peace, before the dark powers of destruction unleashed by science engulf all humanity in planned or accidental self-destruction.

We dare not tempt them with weakness. For only when our arms are sufficient beyond doubt can we be certain beyond doubt that they will never be employed.

But neither can two great and powerful groups of nations take comfort from our present course - both sides overburdened by the cost of modern weapons, both rightly alarmed by the steady spread of the deadly atom, yet both racing to alter that uncertain balance of terror that stays the hand of mankind's final war.

So let us begin anew - remembering on both sides that civility is not a sign of weakness, and sincerity is always subject to proof. Let us never negotiate out of fear. But let us never fear to negotiate.

Let both sides explore what problems unite us instead of belaboring those problems which divide us.

Let both sides, for the first time, formulate serious and precise proposals for the inspection and control of arms - and bring the absolute power to destroy other nations under the absolute control of all nations.

Let both sides seek to invoke the wonders of science instead of its terrors. Together let us explore the stars, conquer the deserts, eradicate disease, tap the ocean depths, and encourage the arts and commerce. Let both sides unite to heed in all corners of the earth the command of Isaiah - to *undo the heavy burdens . . . [and] let the oppressed go free.*

And if a beachhead of cooperation may push back the jungle of suspicion, let both sides join in creating a new endeavor, not a new balance of power, but a new world of law, where the strong are just and the weak secure and the peace preserved.

All this will not be finished in the first one hundred days. Nor will it be finished in the first one thousand days, nor in the life of this Administration, nor even perhaps in our lifetime on this planet. But let us begin.

In your hands, my fellow citizens, more than mine, will rest the final success or failure of our course. Since this country was founded, each generation of Americans has been summoned to give testimony to its national loyalty. The graves of young Americans who answered the call to service surround the globe.

Now the trumpet summons us again - not as a call to bear arms, though arms we need - not as a call to battle, though embattled we are - but a call to bear the burden of a long twilight struggle, year in and year out, *rejoicing in hope, patient in tribulation* - a struggle against the common enemies of man - tyranny, poverty, disease, and war itself.

Can we forge against these enemies a grand and global alliance, North and South, East and West, that can assure a more fruitful life for all mankind? Will you join in that historic effort?

In the long history of the world, only a few generations have been granted the role of defending freedom in its hour of maximum danger. I do not shrink from this responsibility - I welcome it. I do not believe that any of us would exchange places with any other people or any other generation. The energy, the faith, the devotion which we bring to this endeavor will light our country and all who serve it - and the glow from that fire can truly light the world.

And so, my fellow Americans - ask not what your country can do for you - ask what you can do for your country.

My fellow citizens of the world - ask not what America will do for you, but what together we can do for the freedom of man.

Finally, whether you are citizens of America or citizens of the world, ask of us here the same high standards of strength and sacrifice which we ask of you. With a good conscience our only sure reward, with history the final judge of our deeds, let us go forth to lead the land we love, asking His blessing and His help, but knowing that here on earth God's work must truly be our own.

Afterward

On June 26, 1963, at the height of the Cold War, President Kennedy traveled to divided Germany to speak before the Berlin Wall. There he said, *All free men, wherever they may live, are citizens of Berlin, and therefore, as a free man, I take pride in the words, "Ich bin ein Berliner."*

John F. Kennedy was murdered on November 22, 1963.

Selected Reading

Bernstein, Irving, *Promises Kept: John F. Kennedy's New Frontier*, 1991.

Bishop, Jim, *A Day in the Life of President Kennedy*, 1964.

Harrison, Maureen, and Steve Gilbert, Editors, *John F. Kennedy: Word for Word*, 1993.

Reeves, Thomas C., Editor, *John F. Kennedy: The Man, The Politician, The President*, 1990.

Schlesinger, Arthur M., *A Thousand Days: John F. Kennedy in the White House*, 1965.

White, Theodore H., *The Making of the President, 1960*, 1961.

Robert F. Kennedy
The Day Of Affirmation
June 6, 1966

We Americans, like you South Africans, are a people of diverse origins. And we too have a problem, though less difficult than yours, of learning to live together, regardless of origins, in mutual respect for the rights and well-being of all our people.
- Robert F. Kennedy, June 4, 1966

Robert Fitzgerald (*Bobby*) Kennedy was born on November 20, 1925 in Brookline, Massachusetts, the child of Joseph and Rose (Fitzgerald) Kennedy. Educated at Harvard and the University of Virginia Law School, Bobby Kennedy pursued a career in government service, before managing his brother John's successful Presidential campaign. In 1961 President Kennedy appointed his younger brother U.S. Attorney General. After the assassination of his brother, Robert Kennedy won election, in 1964, as Senator from New York. Well known from his time as Attorney General as a friend of oppressed minorities, whether they were African Americans in Mississippi or Mexican Americans in California, in June 1966 Kennedy took his message of racial justice to a place where it had been officially outlawed - South Africa.

From its inception, the Republic of South Africa was a rogue nation for its policy of *apartheid* - state-enforced racial segregation. Robert F. Kennedy, against the wishes of the South African Government, traveled there to speak before white and black student groups. On June 4, 1966, in Johannesburg, South Africa, Bobby Kennedy asked white students - *Suppose God is Black. What if we go to Heaven and we, all our lives, have treated the Negro as inferior, and God is there, and we look up and He is not white. What then is our response?*

On June 6, 1966, before black students in Cape Town, South Africa, Robert F. Kennedy delivered this landmark speech on racial justice, *The Day Of Affirmation*.

Robert F. Kennedy

This is a Day of Affirmation - a celebration of liberty. We stand here in the name of freedom. At the heart of that Western freedom and democracy is the belief that the individual man, the child of God, is the touchstone of value, and all society, all groups, and states, exist for that person's benefit. Therefore the enlargement of liberty for individual human beings must be the supreme goal and the abiding practice of any Western society.

The first element of this individual liberty is the freedom of speech - the right to express and communicate ideas, to set oneself apart from the dumb beasts of field and forest - the right to recall governments to their duties and obligations - above all, the right to affirm one's membership and allegiance to the body politic, to society, to the men with whom we share our land, our heritage, and our children's future.

Hand in hand with freedom of speech goes the power to be heard, to share in the decisions of government which shape men's lives. Everything that makes men's lives worthwhile - family, work, education, a place to rear one's children, and a place to rest one's head - all this depends on the decisions of government; all can be swept away by a government which does not heed the demands of its people, and I mean all of its people. Therefore, the essential humanity of man can be protected and preserved only where the government must answer - not just to the wealthy - not just to those of a particular religion - not just to those of a particular race - but to all of the people.

And even government by the consent of the governed, as in our own Constitution, must be limited in its power to act against its people, so that there may be no interference with the right to worship, but also no interference with the security of the home, no arbitrary imposition of pains or penalties on an ordinary citizen by officials high or low, no restriction on the freedom of men to seek education or to seek work or opportunity of any kind, so that each man may become all that he is capable of becoming.

These are the sacred rights of western society. These were the essential differences between us and Nazi Germany as they were between Athens and Persia.

They are the essences of our differences with communism today. I am unalterably opposed to communism because it exalts the state over the individual and over the family, and because its system contains a lack of freedom of speech, of protest, of religion, and of the press, which is characteristic of a totalitarian regime. The way of opposition to communism, however, is not to imitate its dictatorship, but to enlarge individual human freedom. There are those in every land who would label as *communist* every threat to their privilege. But may I say to you, as I have seen on my travels in all sections of the world, reform is not communism. And the denial of freedom, in whatever name, only strengthens the very communism it claims to oppose.

Many nations have set forth their own definitions and declarations of these principles. And there have often been wide and tragic gaps between promise and performance, ideal and reality. Yet the great ideals have constantly recalled us to our own duties. And, with painful slowness, we in the United States have extended and enlarged the meaning and the practice of freedom to all of our people.

For two centuries, my own country has struggled to overcome the self-imposed handicap of prejudice and discrimination based on nationality, on social class or race, discrimination profoundly repugnant to the theory and to the command of our Constitution. Even as my father grew up in Boston, Massachusetts, signs told him that *No Irish Need Apply*. Two generations later, President Kennedy became the first Irish Catholic, and the first Catholic, to head the nation; but how many men of ability had, before 1961, been denied the opportunity to contribute to the nation's progress because they were Catholic, or because they were of Irish extraction? How many sons of Italian or Jewish or Polish parents slumbered in the slums - untaught, unlearned, their potential lost forever to our nation and to the human race? Even today, what price will we pay before we have assured full opportunity to millions of Negro Americans?

In the last five years we have done more to assure equality to our Negro citizens and to help the deprived, both white and black, than in the hundred years before that time. But much, much more remains to be done.

For there are millions of Negroes untrained for the simplest of jobs, and thousands every day denied their full and equal rights under the law; and the violence of the disinherited, the insulted, and the injured looms over the streets of Harlem and of Watts and Southside Chicago.

But a Negro American trains as an astronaut, one of mankind's first explorers into outer space; another is the chief barrister of the United States government, and dozens sit on the benches of our court; and another, Dr. Martin Luther King, is the second man of African descent to win the Nobel Peace Prize for his non-violent efforts for social justice between all of the races.

We have passed laws prohibiting discrimination in education, in employment, in housing; but these laws alone cannot overcome the heritage of centuries, of broken families and stunted children, and poverty and degradation and pain.

So the road toward equality of freedom is not easy, and great cost and danger march alongside all of us. We are committed to peaceful and non-violent change and that is important for all to understand, though change is unsettling. Still, even in the turbulence of protest and struggle is greater hope for the future, as men learn to claim and achieve for themselves the rights formerly petitioned from others.

And most important of all, all the panoply of government power has been committed to the goal of equality before the law, as we are now committing ourselves to achievement of equal opportunity in fact.

We must recognize the full human equality of all of our people, before God, before the law, and in the councils of government. We must do this, not because it is economically advantageous, although it is - not because the laws of God command it, although they do - not because people in other lands wish it so. We must do it for the single and fundamental reason that it is the right thing to do.

We recognize that there are problems and obstacles before the fulfillment of these ideals in the United States as we recognize that other nations, in Latin America and in Asia and in Africa have their own political, economic, and social problems, their unique barriers to the elimination of injustices.

In some, there is concern that change will submerge the rights of a minority, particularly where that minority is of a different race than that of the majority. We in the United States believe in the protection of minorities; we recognize the contributions that they can make and the leadership they can provide; and we do not believe that any people, whether majority or minority, or individual human beings, are *expendable* in the cause of theory or policy. We recognize also that justice between men and nations is imperfect, and that humanity sometimes progresses very slowly indeed.

All do not develop in the same manner and at the same pace. Nations, like men, often march to the beat of different drummers, and the precise solutions of the United States can neither be dictated nor transplanted to others, and that is not our intention. What is important, however, is that all nations must march toward increasing freedom - toward justice for all - toward a society strong and flexible enough to meet the demands of all of its people, whatever their race, and the demands of a world of immense and dizzying change that face us all.

In a few hours, the plane that brought me to this country crossed over oceans and countries which have been a crucible of human history. In minutes we traced migrations of men over thousands of years - seconds, the briefest glimpse, and we passed battlefields on which millions of men once struggled and died. We could see no national boundaries, no vast gulfs or high walls dividing people from people - only nature and the works of man - homes and factories and farms, everywhere reflecting man's common effort to enrich his life. Everywhere new technology and communications brings men and nations closer together, the concerns of one inevitably become the concerns of all. And our new closeness is stripping away the false masks, the illusion of differences which is at the root of injustice and hate and war. Only earthbound man still clings to the dark and poisoning superstition that his world is bounded by the nearest hill, his universe ends at river's shore, his common humanity is enclosed in the tight circle of those who share his town or his views and the color of his skin.

It is your job, the task of the young people in this world to strip the last remnants of that ancient, cruel belief from the civilization of man.

Each nation has different obstacles and different goals, shaped by the vagaries of history and of experience. Yet as I talk to young people around the world I am impressed not by the diversity but by the closeness of their goals, their desires, and their concerns and their hope for the future. There is discrimination in New York, the racial inequality of apartheid in South Africa, and serfdom in the mountains of Peru. People starve to death in the streets of India; a former Prime Minister is summarily executed in the Congo; intellectuals go to jail in Russia; and thousands are slaughtered in Indonesia; wealth is lavished on armaments everywhere in the world. These are different evils; but they are the common works of man. They reflect the imperfections of human justice, the inadequacy of human compassion, the defectiveness of our sensibility toward the sufferings of our fellows; they mark the limit of our ability to use knowledge for the well-being of our fellow human beings throughout the world. And therefore they call upon common qualities of conscience and indignation, a shared determination to wipe away the unnecessary sufferings of our fellow human beings at home and around the world.

It is these qualities which make of our youth today the only true international community. More than this I think that we could agree on what kind of a world we want to build. It would be a world of independent nations, moving toward international community, each of which protected and respected the basic human freedoms. It would be a world which demanded of each government that it accept its responsibility to insure social justice. It would be a world of constantly accelerating economic progress, not material welfare as an end in and of itself, but as a means to liberate the capacity of every human being to pursue his talents and to pursue his hopes. It would, in short, be a world that we would all be proud to have built.

Just to the north of here are lands of challenge and of opportunity, rich in natural resources, land and minerals and people. Yet they are also lands confronted by the greatest odds - overwhelming ignorance, internal tensions and strife, and great obstacles of climate and geography. Many of these nations, as colonies, were oppressed and were exploited. Yet they have not estranged themselves from the broad traditions of the West; they are hoping and they are gambling their progress and their stability on the chance that we will meet our responsibilities to them, to help them overcome their poverty.

In the world we would like to build, South Africa could play an outstanding role, and a role of leadership in that effort. This country is without question a preeminent repository of the wealth and the knowledge and the skill of the continent. Here are the greater part of Africa's research scientists and steel production, most of its reservoirs of coal and of electric power. Many South Africans have made major contributions to African technical development and world science; the names of some are known wherever men seek to eliminate the ravages of tropical disease and of pestilence. In your faculties and councils, here in this very audience, are hundreds and thousands of men and women who could transform the lives of millions for all time to come.

But the help and leadership of South Africa or of the United States cannot be accepted if we, within our own countries or in our relationships with others, deny individual integrity, human dignity, and the common humanity of man. If we would lead outside our own borders - if we would help those who need our assistance - if we would meet our responsibilities to mankind - we must first, all of us, demolish the borders which history has erected between men within our own nations, barriers of race and religion, social class and ignorance.

Our answer is the world's hope; it is to rely on youth. The cruelties and the obstacles of this swiftly changing planet will not yield to obsolete dogmas and outworn slogans. It cannot be moved by those who cling to a present which is already dying, who prefer the illusion of security to the excitement and danger which comes with even the most peaceful progress. This world demands the qualities of youth - not a time of life but a state of mind, a temper of the will, a quality of imagination, a predominance of courage over timidity, of the appetite for adventure over the life of ease, a man like the Chancellor of this University. It is a revolutionary world that we all live in; and thus, as I have said in Latin America and Asia and in Europe and in my own country, the United States, it is the young people who must take the lead. Thus you, and your young compatriots everywhere have had thrust upon you a greater burden of responsibility than any generation that has ever lived.

There is, said an Italian philosopher, *nothing more difficult to take in hand, more perilous to conduct, or more uncertain in its success than to take the lead in the introduction of a new order of things.* Yet this is the measure of the task of your generation and the road is strewn with many dangers.

First is the danger of futility - the belief there is nothing one man or one woman can do against the enormous array of the world's ills, against misery, against ignorance, or injustice and violence. Yet many of the world's great move ments, of thought and action, have flowed from the work of a single man. A young monk began the Protestant reformation, a young general extended an empire from Macedonia to the borders of the earth, and a young woman reclaimed the territory of France. It was a young Italian explorer who discovered the New World, and 32-year-old Thomas Jefferson who proclaimed that all men are created equal. *Give me a place to stand*, said Archimedes, *and I will move the world.* These men moved the world, and so can we all. Few will have the greatness to bend history; but each of us can work to change a small portion of the events, and in the total of all these acts will be written the history of this generation. Thousands of Peace Corps volunteers are making a difference in the isolated villages and the city slums of dozens of countries. Thousands of unknown men and women in Europe resisted the occupation of the Nazis and many died, but all added to the ultimate strength and freedom of their countries. It is from numberless diverse acts of courage such as these that the belief that human history is thus shaped. Each time a man stands up for an ideal, or acts to improve the lot of others, or strikes out against injustice, he sends forth a tiny ripple of hope, and crossing each other from a million different centers of energy and daring those ripples build a current which can sweep down the mightiest walls of oppression and resistance.

If Athens shall appear great to you, said Pericles, *consider then that her glories were purchased by valiant men, and by men who learned their duty.* That is the source of all greatness in all societies, and it is the key to progress in our own time.

The second danger is that of expediency - of those who say that hopes and beliefs must bend before immediate necessities. Of course if we must act effectively we must deal

with the world as it is. We must get things done. But if
there was one thing that President Kennedy stood for that
touched the most profound feeling of young people across
the world, it was the belief that idealism, high aspiration and
deep convictions are not incompatible with the most practical and efficient of programs - that there is no basic in-
consistency between ideals and realistic possibilities, no
separation between the deepest desires of heart and of
mind and the rational application of human effort to human problems. It is not realistic or hard-headed to solve
problems and take action unguided by ultimate moral aims
and values, although we all know some who claim that it is
so. In my judgment, it is thoughtless folly. For it ignores the
realities of human faith and of passion and of belief - forces
ultimately more powerful than all the calculations of our
economists or of our generals. Of course to adhere to standards, to idealism, to vision in the face of immediate dangers takes great courage and takes self-confidence. But we
also know that only those who dare to fail greatly can ever
achieve greatly.

It is this new idealism which is also, I believe, the common
heritage of a generation which has learned that while effi-
ciency can lead to the camps at Auschwitz, or the streets of
Budapest, only the ideals of humanity and love can climb
the hills of the Acropolis.

A third danger is timidity. Few men are willing to brave the
disapproval of their fellows, the censure of their colleagues,
the wrath of their society. Moral courage is a rarer com-
modity than bravery in battle or great intelligence. Yet it is
the one essential, vital quality for those who seek to change
the world which yields most painfully to change. Aristotle
tells us, *At the Olympic games it is not the finest or the strongest
men who are crowned, but those who enter the lists . . . so too in the*

life of the honorable and the good it is they who act rightly who win the prize. I believe that in this generation those with the courage to enter the conflict will find themselves with companions in every corner of the world.

For the fortunate amongst us, the fourth danger is comfort - the temptation to follow the easy and familiar path of personal ambition and financial success so grandly spread before those who have the privilege of an education. But that is not the road history has marked out for us. There is a Chinese curse which says, *May he live in interesting times.* Like it or not, we live in interesting times. They are times of danger and uncertainty; but they are also the most creative of any time in the history of mankind. And everyone here will ultimately be judged, will ultimately judge himself, on the effort he has contributed to building a new world society and the extent to which his ideals and goals have shaped that effort.

So we part, I to my country and you to remain. We are, if a man of forty can claim the privilege, fellow members of the world's largest younger generation. Each of us have our own work to do. I know at times you must feel very alone with your problems and with your difficulties. But I want to say how impressed I am with what you stand for and for the effort you are making; and I say this not just for myself, but men and women all over the world. And I hope you will often take heart from the knowledge that you are joined with your fellow young people in every land, they struggling with their problems and you with yours, but all joined in a common purpose - that, like the young people of my own country and of every country that I have visited, you are all in many ways more closely united to the brothers of your time than to the older generation in any of these nations; you are determined to build a better future. President Kennedy was speaking to the young people of America, but beyond them to young people everywhere, when he said, *The energy, the faith, the devotion which we bring to this endeavor will light our country and all who serve it - and the glow from that fire can truly light the world.*

And, he added, *With a good conscience our only sure reward, with history the final judge of our deeds, let us go forth and lead the land we love, asking His blessing and His help, but knowing that here on earth God's work must truly be our own.*

I thank you.

Afterward

Robert F. Kennedy was murdered on June 5, 1968. Edward (*Teddy*) Kennedy eulogized his brother, saying, *My brother need not be idealized or enlarged in death beyond what he was in life. He should be remembered simply as a good and decent man who saw wrong and tried to right it, saw suffering and tried to heal it, saw war and tried to stop it. Those of us who loved him and who take him to his rest today pray that what he was to us, and what he wished for others, will some day come to pass for all the world. As he said many times, in many parts of this nation, to those he touched and who sought to touch him, "Some men see things as they are and say why. I dream things that never were and say why not."*

Selected Reading

David, Lester, and Irene David, *Bobby Kennedy: The Making of a Folk Hero*, 1986.

deToledano, Ralph, *The Man Who Would Be President*, 1967.

Dooley, Brian, *Robert Kennedy: The Final Years*, 1996.

Eppridge, Bill, and Hays Gorey, *Robert Kennedy: The Last Campaign*, 1993.

Heymann, C. David, *RFK*, 1998.

Newfield, Jack, *Robert Kennedy: A Memoir*, 1988.

Schlesinger, Arthur, Jr., *Robert Kennedy and His Times*, 1978.

Martin Luther King, Jr.
I Have A Dream
August 28, 1963

Segregation is evil.
- Martin Luther King, Jr., 1956

On December 1, 1955, in Montgomery, Alabama, Rosa Parks, an African American woman, was arrested for her refusal to give up her front seat to a white person and move to the back of a segregated city bus. In response, Montgomery's African American community organized a non-violent boycott against the city's policy of legal segregation. It was led by a local clergyman, Martin Luther King, Jr.

Martin Luther King, Jr. was born on January 15, 1929 in Atlanta, Georgia, the child of Martin, Sr., and Alberta (Williams) King. Following in the footsteps of his father and grandfather, Dr. King studied theology and became a minister. His first pulpit was in Montgomery, Alabama.

The Montgomery Bus Boycott, which made Martin Luther King, Jr. a national figure, ended in December 1956 with the integration of the city bus system. In 1957 Dr. King founded the Southern Christian Leadership Conference (SCLC) to further the civil rights movement through non-violent action. In the tumultuous years that followed, Dr. King led major civil rights protests throughout the South, including Selma, Alabama - *I don't march because I like it; I march because I must!* - and Birmingham, Alabama - *I would rather stay in jail the rest of my life than make a butchery of my conscience.* In 1964 Dr. King, in recognition of his work, was awarded the Nobel Peace Prize - *History has thrust me into this position. It would be immoral and a sign of ingratitude if I did not face my moral responsibility to do what I can in this struggle.*

On August 28, 1963, speaking on the steps of the Lincoln Memorial before a crowd of over 200,000, Martin Luther King, Jr. delivered this landmark speech, *I Have A Dream.*

Martin Luther King, Jr.

I am happy to join with you today in what will go down in history as the greatest demonstration for freedom in the history of our nation.

Fivescore years ago, a great American, in whose symbolic shadow we stand today, signed the Emancipation Proclamation. This momentous decree came as a great beacon light of hope to millions of Negro slaves who had been seared in the flames of withering injustice. It came as a joyous daybreak to end the long night of their captivity.

But one hundred years later, the Negro still is not free; one hundred years later, the life of the Negro is still sadly crippled by the manacles of segregation and the chains of discrimination; one hundred years later, the Negro lives on a lonely island of poverty in the midst of a vast ocean of material prosperity; one hundred years later, the Negro is still languished in the corners of American society and finds himself in exile in his own land.

So we've come here today to dramatize a shameful condition. In a sense we've come to our nation's capital to cash a check. When the architects of our republic wrote the magnificent words of the Constitution and the Declaration of Independence, they were signing a promissory note to which every American was to fall heir. This note was the promise that all men, yes, black men as well as white men, would be guaranteed the unalienable rights of life, liberty, and the pursuit of happiness.

It is obvious today that America has defaulted on this promissory note in so far as her citizens of color are concerned. Instead of honoring this sacred obligation, America has given the Negro people a bad check, a check which has come back marked *insufficient funds*. We refuse to believe that there are insufficient funds in the great vaults of opportunity of this nation. And so we've come to cash this check, a check that will give us upon demand the riches of freedom and the security of justice.

We have also come to this hallowed spot to remind America of the fierce urgency of now. This is no time to engage in the luxury of cooling off or to take the tranquilizing drug of gradualism. Now is the time to make real the promises of democracy; now is the time to rise from the dark and desolate valley of segregation to the sunlit path of racial justice; now is the time to lift our nation from the quicksands of racial injustice to the solid rock of brotherhood; now is the time to make justice a reality for all God's children. It would be fatal for the nation to overlook the urgency of the moment. This sweltering summer of the Negro's legitimate discontent will not pass until there is an invigorating autumn of freedom and equality.

Nineteen sixty-three is not an end, but a beginning. And those who hope that the Negro needed to blow off steam and will now be content, will have a rude awakening if the nation returns to business as usual.

There will be neither rest nor tranquillity in America until the Negro is granted his citizenship rights. The whirlwinds of revolt will continue to shake the foundations of our nation until the bright day of justice emerges.

But there is something that I must say to my people who stand on the warm threshold which leads into the palace of justice. In the process of gaining our rightful place we must not be guilty of wrongful deeds.

Let us not seek to satisfy our thirst for freedom by drinking from the cup of bitterness and hatred. We must forever conduct our struggle on the high plane of dignity and discipline. We must not allow our creative protest to degenerate into physical violence. Again and again we must rise to the majestic heights of meeting physical force with soul force.

The marvelous new militancy which has engulfed the Negro community must not lead us to a distrust of all white people, for many of our white brothers, as evidenced by their presence here today, have come to realize that their destiny is tied up with our destiny and they have come to realize that their freedom is inextricably bound to our freedom. This offense we share mounted to storm the battlements of injustice must be carried forth by a biracial army. We cannot walk alone.

And as we walk, we must make the pledge that we shall always march ahead. We cannot turn back. There are those who are asking the devotees of civil rights, *When will you be satisfied?* We can never be satisfied as long as the Negro is the victim of the unspeakable horrors of police brutality.

We can never be satisfied as long as our bodies, heavy with fatigue of travel, cannot gain lodging in the motels of the highways and the hotels of the cities. We cannot be satisfied as long as the Negro's basic mobility is from a smaller ghetto to a larger one.

We can never be satisfied as long as our children are stripped of their selfhood and robbed of their dignity by signs stating *for whites only*. We cannot be satisfied as long as a Negro in Mississippi cannot vote and a Negro in New York believes he has nothing for which to vote. No, we are not satisfied, and we will not be satisfied until justice rolls down like waters and righteousness like a mighty stream.

I am not unmindful that some of you have come here out of excessive trials and tribulation. Some of you have come fresh from narrow jail cells. Some of you have come from areas where your quest for freedom left you battered by the storms of persecution and staggered by the winds of police brutality. You have been the veterans of creative suffering. Continue to work with the faith that unearned suffering is redemptive.

Go back to Mississippi; go back to Alabama; go back to South Carolina; go back to Georgia; go back to Louisiana; go back to the slums and ghettos of the northern cities, knowing that somehow this situation can, and will be changed. Let us not wallow in the valley of despair.

So I say to you, my friends, that even though we must face the difficulties of today and tomorrow, I still have a dream. It is a dream deeply rooted in the American dream that one day this nation will rise up and live out the true meaning of its creed - we hold these truths to be self-evident, that all men are created equal.

I have a dream that one day on the red hills of Georgia, sons of former slaves and sons of former slave-owners will be able to sit down together at the table of brotherhood.

I have a dream that one day, even the state of Mississippi, a state sweltering with the heat of injustice, sweltering with the heat of oppression, will be transformed into an oasis of freedom and justice.

I have a dream my four little children will one day live in a nation where they will not be judged by the color of their skin but by content of their character. I have a dream to-day!

I have a dream that one day, down in Alabama, with its vicious racists, with its governor having his lips dripping with the words of interposition and nullification, that one day, right there in Alabama, little black boys and black girls will be able to join hands with little white boys and white girls as sisters and brothers. I have a dream today!

I have a dream that one day every valley shall be exalted, every hill and mountain shall be made low, the rough places shall be made plain, and the crooked places shall be made straight and the glory of the Lord will be revealed and all flesh shall see it together.

This is our hope. This is the faith that I go back to the South with.

With this faith we will be able to hear out of the mountain of despair a stone of hope. With this faith we will be able to transform the jangling discords of our nation into a beautiful symphony of brotherhood.

With this faith we will be able to work together, to pray together, to struggle together, to go to jail together, to stand up for freedom together, knowing that we will be free one day. This will be the day when all of God's children will be able to sing with new meaning - *my country 'tis of thee; sweet land of liberty; of thee I sing; land where my fathers died, land of the pilgrim's pride; from every mountain side, let freedom ring* - and if America is to be a great nation, this must become true.

So let freedom ring from the prodigious hilltops of New Hampshire.

Let freedom ring from the mighty mountains of New York.

Let freedom ring from the heightening Alleghenies of Pennsylvania.

Let freedom ring from the snow-capped Rockies of Colorado.

Let freedom ring from the curvaceous slopes of California.

But not only that.

Let freedom ring from Stone Mountain of Georgia.

Let freedom ring from Lookout Mountain of Tennessee.

Let freedom ring from every hill and molehill of Mississippi; from every mountainside, let freedom ring.

And when we allow freedom to ring, when we let it ring from every village and hamlet, from every state and city, we will be able to speed up that day when all of God's children - black men and white men, Jews and Gentiles, Catholics and Protestants - will be able to join hands and to sing in the words of the old Negro spiritual, *Free at last, free at last; thank God Almighty, we are free at last.*

Afterward

On April 3, 1968, in Memphis, Tennessee, where he was leading another protest, Dr. King said, *I've seen the promised land. I may not get there with you. But I want you to know tonight, that we as a people will get to the promised land.* The next day, April 4, 1968, Martin Luther King, Jr. was murdered.

Selected Reading

Bishop, Jim, *The Days of Martin Luther King, Jr.*, 1971.

Colaiaco, James A., *Martin Luther King, Jr.: Apostle of Militant Nonviolence*, 1993.

Davis, Lenwood G., *I Have a Dream: The Life and Times of Martin Luther King, Jr.*, 1973.

Garrow, David, *Bearing The Cross*, 1986.

King, Coretta Scott, *My Life With Martin Luther King, Jr.*, 1993.

King, Martin Luther, Jr., *The Autobiography of Martin Luther King, Jr.*, 1998.

Oates, Stephen B., *Let The Trumpet Sound: A Life of Martin Luther King, Jr.*, 1994.

Douglas MacArthur
Old Soldiers Never Die
April 19, 1951

In war there can be no substitute for victory.
- General Douglas MacArthur, 1951

Douglas MacArthur was born on January 26, 1880 at the Army barracks in Little Rock, Arkansas, the son of General Arthur and Mary (Hardy) MacArthur. Educated at West Point, MacArthur served in World War I, as West Point Superintendent (1919-25), Army Chief of Staff (1930-35), and Military Advisor to the Philippines (1935-41). In World War II, he served as Commander-in-Chief of the Allied Forces in the Pacific. In 1942 MacArthur promised the Philippines *I shall return* and in 1945, after conducting one of the greatest military campaigns ever waged, he fulfilled his promise, proclaiming, *I have returned*. On September 2, 1945, MacArthur accepted the surrender of Japan. He then served (1945-51) as the Supreme Allied Commander of the defeated Japanese nation.

On June 25, 1950, North Korea, aided by China, invaded South Korea. President Truman placed General MacArthur in charge of the U.S./U.N. forces. After nearly a year of indecisive fighting, MacArthur secretly urged the President to allow him to attack China. The President, who was committed to a limited war and a negotiated truce, refused. On April 5, 1951, the General defied the President and went public with his complaints - *There is nothing to negotiate about. We must win. There is no substitute for victory.* On April 11, 1951, President Truman fired General MacArthur for insubordination. The nation erupted in pro-MacArthur protests. A *MacArthur For President* movement began.

On April 19, 1951, Douglas MacArthur, who had returned to Washington, D.C. to a tumultuous hero's welcome, addressed a Joint Session of Congress and delivered this landmark speech, *Old Soldiers Never Die*.

Mr. President, Mr. Speaker, and distinguished members of the Congress, I stand on this rostrum with a sense of deep humility and great pride - humility in the wake of those great American architects of our history who have stood here before me, pride in the reflection that this home of legislative debate represents human liberty in the purest form yet devised. Here are centered the hopes and aspirations and faith of the entire human race.

I do not stand here as advocate for any partisan cause, for the issues are fundamental and reach quite beyond the realm of partisan considerations. They must be resolved on the highest plane of national interest if our course is to prove sound and our future protected. I trust, therefore, that you will do me the justice of receiving that which I have to say as solely expressing the considered viewpoint of a fellow American. I address you with neither rancor nor bitterness in the fading twilight of life, with but one purpose in mind - to serve my country.

The issues are global, and so interlocked that to consider the problems of one sector oblivious to those of another is to court disaster for the whole. While Asia is commonly referred to as the gateway to Europe, it is no less true that Europe is the gateway to Asia, and the broad influence of the one cannot fail to have its impact upon the other.

There are those who claim our strength is inadequate to protect on both fronts, that we cannot divide our effort. I can think of no greater expression of defeatism. If a potential enemy can divide his strength on two fronts, it is for us to counter his efforts. The Communist threat is a global one. Its successful advance in one sector threatens the destruction of every other sector. You cannot appease or otherwise surrender to communism in Asia without simultaneously undermining our efforts to halt its advance in Europe.

... I now turn to the Korean conflict. While I was not consulted prior to the President's decision to intervene in support of the Republic of Korea, that decision, from a military standpoint, proved a sound one. As I say, it proved a sound one, as we hurled back the invader and decimated his forces. Our victory was complete, and our objectives within reach, when Red China intervened with numerically superior ground forces. This created a new war and an entirely new situation, a situation not contemplated when our forces were committed against the North Korean invaders - a situation which called for new decisions in the diplomatic sphere to permit the realistic adjustment of military strategy. Such decisions have not been forthcoming.

While no man in his right mind would advocate sending our ground forces into continental China, and such was never given a thought, the new situation did urgently demand a drastic revision of strategic planning if our political aim was to defeat this new enemy as we had defeated the old.

Apart from the military need, as I saw it, to neutralize the sanctuary protection given the enemy north of the Yalu, I felt that military necessity in the conduct of the war made necessary -

One. The intensification of our economic blockade against China.

Two. The imposition of a naval blockade against the China coast.

Three. Removal of restrictions on air reconnaissance of China's coastal area and of Manchuria.

Four. Removal of restrictions on the forces of the Republic of China on Formosa, with logistical support to contribute to their effective operations against the Chinese mainland.

For entertaining these views - all professionally designed to support our forces committed to Korea and bring hostilities to an end with the least possible delay and at a saving of countless American and Allied lives - I have been severely criticized in lay circles, principally abroad, despite my understanding that from a military standpoint the above views have been fully shared in the past by practically every military leader concerned with the Korean campaign, including our own Joint Chiefs of Staff.

I called for reinforcements, but was informed that reinforcements were not available. I made clear that if not permitted to destroy the enemy built-up bases north of the Yalu, if not permitted to utilize the friendly Chinese force of some 600,000 men on Formosa, if not permitted to blockade the China coast to prevent the Chinese Reds from getting succor from without, and if there were to be no hope of major reinforcements, the position of the command from the military standpoint forbade victory.

We could hold in Korea by constant maneuver and at an approximate area where our supply line advantages were in balance with the supply line disadvantages of the enemy, but we could hope at best for only an indecisive campaign with its terrible and constant attrition upon our forces if the enemy utilized his full military potential.

I have constantly called for the new political decisions essential to a solution. Efforts have been made to distort my position. It has been said in effect that I was a warmonger. Nothing could be further from the truth. I know war as few other men now living know it, and nothing to me is more revolting. I have long advocated its complete abolition, as its very destructiveness on both friend and foe has rendered it useless as a means of settling international disputes.

Indeed, on the second day of September, 1945, just following the surrender of the Japanese nation on the battleship *Missouri*, I formally cautioned as follows,

> *Men since the beginning of time have sought peace. Various methods through the ages have been attempted to devise an international process to prevent or settle disputes between nations. From the very start workable methods were found insofar as individual citizens were concerned, but the mechanics of an instrumentality of larger international scope have never been successful.*
>
> *Military alliances, balances of power, leagues of nations, all in turn failed, leaving the only path to be by way of the crucible of war. The utter destructiveness of war now blocks out this alternative. We have had our last chance. If we will not devise some greater and more equitable system, our Armageddon will be at our door. The problem basically is theological and involves a spiritual recrudescence, an improvement of human character that will synchronize with our almost matchless advances in science, art, literature, and all material and cultural developments of the past 2,000 years. It must be of the spirit if we are to save the flesh.*

But once war is forced upon us, there is no other alternative than to apply every available means to bring it to a swift end. War's very object is victory, not prolonged indecision. In war there is no substitute for victory.

There are some who for varying reasons would appease Red China. They are blind to history's clear lesson, for history teaches with unmistakable emphasis that appeasement but begets new and bloodier war. It points to no single instance where this end has justified that means, where appeasement has led to more than a sham peace.

Like blackmail, it lays the basis for new and successively greater demands until, as in blackmail, violence becomes the only other alternative. Why, my soldiers asked of me, surrender military advantages to an enemy in the field? I could not answer.

Some may say to avoid spread of the conflict into an all-out war with China, others, to avoid Soviet intervention. Neither explanation seems valid, for China is already engaging with the maximum power it can commit, and the Soviet will not necessarily mesh its actions with our moves. Like a cobra, any new enemy will more likely strike whenever it feels that the relativity in military or other potential is in its favor on a worldwide basis.

The tragedy of Korea is further heightened by the fact that its military action is confined to its territorial limits. It condemns that nation, which it is our purpose to save, to suffer the devastating impact of full naval and air bombardment while the enemy's sanctuaries are fully protected from such attack and devastation. Of the nations of the world, Korea alone, up to now, is the sole one which has risked its all against communism. The magnificence of the courage and fortitude of the Korean people defies description. They have chosen to risk death rather than slavery. Their last words to me were, *Don't scuttle the Pacific.*

I have just left your fighting sons in Korea. They have met all tests there, and I can report to you without reservation that they are splendid in every way. It was my constant effort to preserve them and end this savage conflict honorably and with the least loss of time and a minimum sacrifice of life. Its growing bloodshed has caused me the deepest anguish and anxiety. Those gallant men will remain often in my thoughts and in my prayers always.

the first great televised speeches, was interrupted continually by wild applause and standing ovations. The Speaker of the House reported, *When MacArthur finished there wasn't a dry eye in the House.* After losing the 1952 Republican Presidential nomination to America's only other five-star General, Dwight D. Eisenhower, MacArthur went into a secluded retirement. On May 12, 1962 MacArthur returned to West Point and told the cadets, *The shadows are lengthening for me. The twilight is here. My days of old have vanished - tone and tints. They have gone glimmering through the dreams of things that were. Their memory is one of wondrous beauty, watered by tears and coaxed and caressed by the smiles of yesterday. I listen then, but with thirsty ear, for the witching melody of faint bugles blowing reveille, of far drums beating the long roll. In my dreams I hear again the crash of guns, the rattle of musketry, the strange, mournful mutter of the battlefield. But in the evening of my memory I come back to West Point. Always there echoes and re-echoes - Duty, Honor, Country.*

Douglas MacArthur died on April 5, 1964.

Selected Reading

Archer, Jules, *Front-Line General: Douglas MacArthur*, 1965.
Blair, Clay, Jr., *MacArthur*, 1977.
Kelley, Frank R., and Cornelius Ryan, *MacArthur: A Biography*, 1951.
MacArthur, Douglas, *Reminiscences*, 1964.
Manchester, William R., *American Caesar*, 1983.
Perret, Geoffrey, *Old Soldiers Never Die*, 1996.
Whitney, Courtney, *MacArthur: His Rendezvous With History*, 1956.
Willoughby, Charles A., and John Chamberlain, *MacArthur, 1941-1951*, 1956.

George Marshall
The Marshall Plan
June 5, 1947

The greatest American soldier.
- President Harry Truman

So long as hunger, poverty, desperation, and resulting chaos threaten the people of Western Europe, some 270 millions, there will surely develop social unease and political unrest.
- Secretary of State George Marshall, 1947

George Catlett Marshall, Jr. was born on December 31, 1880 in Uniontown, Pennsylvania, the son of George, Sr. and Laura (Bradford) Marshall. Educated at the Virginia Military Academy, Marshall entered the U.S. Army in 1902, serving in World War I, and afterwards at the Army's War College, Infantry School, and War Plans Division. On September 1, 1939, the day World War II began, President Franklin Roosevelt appointed Marshall Army Chief of Staff. Marshall immediately began to prepare the Army, then a fighting force of only 175,000 soldiers, for a possible war in Europe. After the Japanese attack on Pearl Harbor on December 7, 1941, Marshall counseled President Roosevelt to adopt a *Europe First* strategy, concentrating America's primary war effort on the defeat of Germany. After the defeat of Germany, Winston Churchill called Marshall *the organizer of victory.* In 1947 President Truman appointed George Marshall U.S. Secretary of State.

At the end of World War II, Western Europe was in ruins. To stop their desperate situation from leading to yet another war, the United States prepared a massive economic assistance plan to rebuild Europe.

On June 5, 1947, at Harvard University, Secretary of State George Marshall delivered this landmark speech, outlining the European Recovery Program, which the world came to know as *The Marshall Plan.*

106

I need not tell you gentlemen that the world situation is very serious. That must be apparent to all intelligent people. I think one difficulty is that the problem is one of such enormous complexity that the very mass of facts presented to the public by press and radio make it exceedingly difficult for the man in the street to reach a clear appraisement of the situation. Furthermore, the people of this country are distant from the troubled areas of the earth and it is hard for them to comprehend the plight and consequent reactions of the long-suffering peoples, and the effect of those reactions on their governments in connection with our efforts to promote peace in the world.

In considering the requirements for the rehabilitation of Europe, the physical loss of life, the visible destruction of cities, factories, mines, and railroads was correctly estimated, but it has become obvious during recent months that this visible destruction was probably less serious than the dislocation of the entire fabric of [the] European economy. For the past ten years, conditions have been highly abnormal. The feverish preparation for war and the more feverish maintenance of the war effort engulfed all aspects of national economics. Machinery has fallen into disrepair or is entirely obsolete. Under the arbitrary and destructive Nazi rule, virtually every possible enterprise was geared into the German war machine. Long-standing commercial ties, private institutions, banks, insurance companies, and shipping companies disappeared, through loss of capital, absorption, through nationalization, or by simple destruction. In many countries, confidence in the local currency has been severely shaken. The breakdown of the business structure of Europe during the war was complete. Recovery has been seriously retarded by the fact that two years after the close of hostilities a peace settlement with Germany and Austria has not been agreed upon. But even given a more prompt solution of these difficult problems, the rehabilitation of the economic structure of Europe quite evidently will require a much longer time and greater effort than had been foreseen.

There is a phase of this matter which is both interesting and serious. The farmer has always produced the foodstuffs to exchange with the city dweller for the other necessities of life. This division of labor is the basis of modern civilization. At the present time it is threatened with breakdown. The town and city industries are not producing adequate goods to exchange with the food-producing farmer. Raw materials and fuel are in short supply. Machinery is lacking or worn out. The farmer or the peasant cannot find the goods for sale which he desires to purchase. So the sale of his farm produce for money which he cannot use seems to him an unprofitable transaction. He, therefore, has withdrawn many fields from crop cultivation and is using them for grazing. He feeds more grain to stock and finds for himself and his family an ample supply of food, however short he may be on clothing and the other ordinary gadgets of civilization. Meanwhile people in the cities are short of food and fuel. So the governments are forced to use their foreign money and credits to procure these necessities abroad. This process exhausts funds which are urgently needed for reconstruction. Thus a very serious situation is rapidly developing which bodes no good for the world. The modern system of the division of labor upon which the exchange of products is based is in danger of breaking down.

The truth of the matter is that Europe's requirements for the next three or four years of foreign food and other essential products - principally from America - are so much greater than her present ability to pay that she must have substantial additional help, or face economic, social, and political deterioration of a very grave character.

The remedy lies in breaking the vicious circle and restoring the confidence of the European people in the economic future of their own countries and of Europe as a whole. The manufacturer and the farmer throughout wide areas must be able and willing to exchange their products for currencies the continuing value of which is not open to question.

Aside from the demoralizing effect on the world at large and the possibilities of disturbances arising as a result of the desperation of the people concerned, the consequences to the economy of the United States should be apparent to all. It is logical that the United States should do whatever it is able to do to assist in the return of normal economic health in the world, without which there can be no political stability and no assured peace. Our policy is directed not against any country or doctrine but against hunger, poverty, desperation, and chaos. Its purpose should be the revival of a working economy in the world so as to permit the emergence of political and social conditions in which free institutions can exist. Such assistance, I am convinced, must not be on a piecemeal basis as various crises develop. Any assistance that this Government may render in the future should provide a cure rather than a mere palliative. Any government that is willing to assist in the task of recovery will find full cooperation, I am sure, on the part of the United States Government. Any government which maneuvers to block the recovery of other countries cannot expect help from us. Furthermore, governments, political parties, or groups which seek to perpetuate human misery in order to profit therefrom politically or otherwise will encounter the opposition of the United States.

It is already evident that, before the United States Government can proceed much further in its efforts to alleviate the situation and help start the European world on its way to recovery, there must be some agreement among the countries of Europe as to the requirements of the situation and the part those countries themselves will take in order to give proper effect to whatever action might be undertaken by this Government. It would be neither fitting nor efficacious for this Government to undertake to draw up unilaterally a program designed to place Europe on its feet economically. This is the business of the Europeans. The initiative, I think, must come from Europe. The role of this country should consist of friendly aid in the drafting of a European program and of later support of such a program so far as it may be practical for us to do so. The program should be a joint one, agreed to by a number, if not all European nations.

An essential part of any successful action on the part of the United States is an understanding on the part of the people of America of the character of the problem and the remedies to be applied. Political passion and prejudice should have no part. With foresight, and a willingness on the part of our people to face up to the vast responsibility which history has clearly placed upon our country, the difficulties I have outlined can and will be overcome.

Afterward

The Marshall Plan, America's multi-billion dollar investment in post-war Europe, physically rebuilt and politically stabilized Western Europe. For his efforts, George Marshall was awarded the 1953 Nobel Peace Prize. Upon receiving the Prize Marshall said, *There has been considerable comment over awarding the Nobel Peace Prize to a soldier. I am afraid it does not seem so remarkable to me. The cost of war is constantly spread before me, written neatly in many ledgers whose columns are gravestones. I am greatly moved to find some means or method of avoiding another calamity of war.*

George Marshall died on October 16, 1959.

Selected Reading

Cray, Ed, *General of the Army: George C. Marshall, Soldier and Statesman,* 1990.

Pogue, Forrest C., *George C. Marshall,* 1987.

Stoler, Mark A., *George C. Marshall: Soldier-Statesman of the American Century,* 1989.

Wilson, Rose Page, *General Marshall Remembered,* 1968.

Joseph McCarthy
The Witch Hunt
February 9, 1950

When I was a small boy on the farm, mother raised chickens. We lived fairly close to the woods, and snakes and skunks would steal the baby chicks from the mother and kill them. One of the jobs I had was to dig out and destroy those killers. It was not a pleasant job and sometimes we did not smell too good when the job was finished. But the skunks were dead and the chickens were alive. A much more dangerous and smellier breed of skunk is now being dug out of Washington. And to those of you who do not like rough tactics - any farm boy can tell you that there is no dainty way of clubbing the fangs off a rattler or killing a skunk. **- Senator Joseph McCarthy**

In the early 1950's, a Cold War *Red Hysteria*, the fear of Communists inside the United States Government, gripped the nation. The question - *Are you now, or have you ever been, a member of the Communist Party?* - echoed through Congress. The man asking the question was Senator Joseph McCarthy.

Joseph Raymond McCarthy was born on November 14, 1908 near Appleton, Wisconsin, the child of Timothy and Bridget (Tierney) McCarthy. Educated at Marquette University, McCarthy earned a law degree. In 1946, calling himself *Tail-Gunner Joe,* a reference to his claim of having flown dangerous combat missions in the South Pacific, when in fact he had been assigned a desk job, Joseph McCarthy ran as the Republican candidate for the U.S. Senate from Wisconsin, winning the election by smearing his opponent as a *Communist fellow-traveler.* In the U.S. Senate McCarthy won the reputation as a fervent anti-Communist crusader - *We cannot blind our eyes to the fact that we are engaged in a final, all-out battle between Communist atheism and Christian democracy.*

On February 9, 1950, speaking in Wheeling, West Virginia, Senator Joseph McCarthy shocked the nation by charging that he had a list of *205 Communists* in the U.S. State Department, in this landmark speech, *The Witch Hunt.*

Joseph McCarthy

(No transcript of this speech survives. This version is based on the best available information we have been able to obtain. - The Editors)

Five years after a world war has been won, men's hearts should anticipate a long peace, and men's minds should be free from the heavy weight that comes with war. But this is not such a period - for this is not a period of peace. This is a time of the *cold war*. This is a time when all the world is split into two vast, increasingly hostile armed camps, a time of a great armaments race. Today we can almost physically hear the mutterings and rumblings of an invigorated god of war. You can see it, feel it, and hear it all the way from the hills of Indochina, from the shores of Formosa, right over into the very heart of Europe itself.

The one encouraging thing is that the *mad moment* has not yet arrived for the firing of the gun or the exploding of the bomb which will set civilization about the final task of destroying itself. There is still a hope for peace if we finally decide that no longer can we safely blind our eyes and close our ears to those facts which are shaping up more and more clearly. And that is that we are now engaged in a showdown fight, not the usual war between nations for land areas or other material gains but a war between two diametrically opposed ideologies.

The real, basic difference lies in the religion of immoralism - invented by Marx, preached feverishly by Lenin, and carried to the unimaginable extremes by Stalin. This religion of immoralism, if the Red half of the world wins, and well it may, this religion of immoralism will more deeply wound and damage mankind than any conceivable economic or political system.

Karl Marx dismissed God as a hoax, and Lenin and Stalin have added in clear-cut, unmistakable language their resolve

113

that no nation, no people who believe in a God can exist side by side with their communistic state.

Today we are engaged in a final, all-out battle between communistic atheism and Christianity. The modern champions of Communism have selected this as the time. And, ladies and gentlemen, the chips are down, they are truly down.

Ladies and gentlemen, can there be anyone here tonight who is so blind as to say that the war is not on? Can there be anyone who fails to realize that the Communist world has said, *The time is now* - this is the time for the show-down between the democratic Christian world and the Communist atheistic world? Unless we face this fact, we shall pay the price that must be paid by those who wait too long.

At war's end we were physically the strongest nation on earth and, at least potentially, the most powerful intellectually and morally. Ours could have been the honor of being a beacon in the desert of destruction, a shining, living proof that civilization was not yet ready to destroy itself. Unfortunately, we have failed miserably and tragically to arise to the opportunity.

The reason why we find ourselves in a position of impotency is not because our only powerful, potential enemy has sent men to invade our shores, but rather because of the traitorous actions of those who have been treated so well by this nation. It has not been the less fortunate or members of minority groups who have been selling this nation out, but rather those who have had all the benefits that the wealthiest nation on earth has had to offer, the finest homes, the finest college education, and the finest jobs in government we can give.

This is glaringly true in the State Department. There the bright young men who are born with silver spoons in their mouths are the ones who have been worst.

In my opinion the State Department, which is one of the most important government departments, is thoroughly infested with Communists.

And, ladies and gentlemen, while I cannot take the time to name all the men in the State Department who have been named as active members of the Communist Party and members of a spy ring, I have here in my hand a list of 205 names that were made known to the Secretary of State as being members of the Communist Party and who nevertheless are still working and shaping policy in the State Department.

One thing to remember in discussing the Communists in our government is that we are not dealing with spies who get thin pieces of silver to steal the blueprints of new weapons. We are dealing with a far more sinister type of activity because it permits the enemy to guide and shape our policy.

Actually, ladies and gentlemen, one of the important reasons for the graft, the corruption, the dishonesty, the disloyalty, the treason in high government positions - one of the most important reasons why it continues - is a lack of moral uprising on the part of the 140 million American people. In the light of history, however, this is not hard to explain.

It is the result of an emotional hangover and a temporary moral lapse which follows every war. It is the apathy to evil which people who have been subjected to the tremendous evils of war feel. As the people of the world see mass murder, the destruction of defenseless and innocent people and all of the crime and lack of morals which go with war, they become numb and apathetic. It has always been thus after war. However, the morals of our people have not been destroyed. They still exist. This cloak of numbness and apathy has only needed a spark to rekindle them. Happily, this spark has finally been supplied.

As you know, very recently the Secretary of State [Dean Acheson] proclaimed his loyalty to a man [Alger Hiss] guilty of what has always been considered as the most abominable of all crimes, of being a traitor to the people who gave him a position of great trust. The Secretary of State, in attempting to justify his continued devotion to the man who sold out the Christian world to the atheistic world, referred to Christ's Sermon on the Mount as a justification and reason therefor, and the reaction of the American people to this would have made the heart of Abraham Lincoln happy. When this pompous diplomat in striped pants, with a phony British accent, proclaimed to the American people that Christ on the Mount endorsed communism, high treason, and betrayal of a sacred trust, the blasphemy was so great that it awakened the dormant indignation of the American people.

He has lighted the spark which is resulting in a moral uprising and will end only when the whole sorry mess of twisted, warped thinkers are swept from the national scene so that we may have a new birth of national honesty and decency in government.

Joseph McCarthy

Afterward

In 1954, the U.S. Senate censured Senator McCarthy for bringing upon the Senate *dishonor and disrepute. Joseph McCarthy, by his reckless charges, has so preyed upon the fears, hatreds, and prejudices of the American people that he has started a prairie fire which neither he nor anyone else may be able to control.*

Joseph McCarthy died on May 2, 1957.

Selected Reading

Anderson, Jack, *McCarthy, The Man, The Senator, The "Ism"*, 1953.

Oshinsky, David. *A Conspiracy So Immense: The World of Joe McCarthy*, 1983.

Potter, Charles E., *Days of Shame*, 1971.

Reeves, Thomas, *The Life and Times of Joe McCarthy*, 1997.

Carry Nation
Thou Shalt Not Drink
September 1, 1901

I smashed the Kansas saloons to arouse the people. If some ordinary means had been used, people would have heard and forgotten, but the strange act of smashing demanded an explanation and the people wanted that. They will never stop talking about this until the question of Prohibition is settled. **- Carry Nation, 1905**

On June 7, 1900, Carry Nation, a 53-year-old grandmother, entered a saloon in Kiowa, Kansas, with a hatchet and yelled, *Men! I have come to save you from a drunkard's grave!* She smashed the liquor bottles behind the bar to pieces, and then moved on to another saloon. The saloons of Kiowa were soon closed. *Mother Nation* soon took her *Saloon Smashing Crusade* to Wichita, Topeka, and Kansas City - *People of Kansas! This is the right arm of God! I am destined to wreck every saloon in this State!*

Carry Amelia Moore was born on November 25, 1846 in Garrard County, Kentucky, the child of George and Mary (Campbell) Moore. In 1877 Carry Moore, after a disastrous first marriage to an alcoholic, married a minister, David Nation, and settled in Barber County, Kansas. Although Kansas was by law a *dry state* (its Constitution's Prohibition Clause made it a crime to sell alcohol), there were illegal saloons everywhere. In 1892 Carry Nation joined the Women's Christian Temperance Union's Barber County Chapter but found their non-confrontational tactics were too mild. She began her own *Saloon-Smashing Crusade*, which made her famous. Her lecture tours, where she appeared on stage with a hatchet in one hand and a Bible in the other, drew huge crowds and served to further advance the cause of national prohibition.

On September 1, 1901, in New York City's Carnegie Hall, and thereafter for the next ten years, Carry Nation delivered this landmark temperance lecture, *Thou Shalt Not Drink*.

God is a politician; so is the Devil. God's politics are to protect and defend mankind, bringing to them the highest good and finally heaven. The Devil's politics are to deceive, degrade, and to make miserable, finally ending in hell. The Bible fully explains this. The two kinds of seed started out from Abel and Cain, then Ishmael and Isaac, Esau and Jacob. There are but these two kinds of people. God's crowd and the Devil's crowd.

The first law given and broken in Eden was a prohibition law. God said, *Thou shalt not.* The devil tempted and persuaded the first pair to disobey. He did it by deceiving the woman. The fact of redemption now is to bring them back to the law of God. What is law? God says that sin is a transgression of law. Blackstone says, *Law commands that which is right and prohibits that which is wrong.* Law is one, as truth is one. It is not possible to make a bad law. If it is bad, it is not a law. We have bad statutes. Law is always right. Nothing is wrong that is legal, and wrong may be licensed, but never legalized. I find lawyers who do not understand this. I often hear the term *legalized saloon.*

When I was passing the building of the Supreme Court in New York City, on Madison Avenue, I read an inscription on one of the marble statues representing a judge with a book on either side of the door, *Every law not based on wisdom is a menace to the state.* This is a false, misleading sentence for all law is wisdom. It might have read, *All statutes not based on wisdom are a menace to the state.* Then at the base of the statue of a soldier, on the other side of the entrance, was this statement, *We do not use force until good laws are defied,* which ought to read, *We do not use force until laws are defied.* Such ideas as these are corrupting courts, and biasing the public mind, and the injury is more than apparent to the observer. If law is not a standard, what standard can we have? We must have one. We repeat again, *Law commands that which is right and prohibits that which is wrong.* Any statute that does this is lawful. Any that does not is anarchy.

God is truly the author of law. The theocratic form of government was perfect and the only perfect government that ever existed; we need no other statutes than those that God gave. He said, *We must not kill a bird sitting on her young, must not see our enemy's beast fall under his burden and not help him rise.* And the refinement of mercy was taught in the statute that said, *You must not kill the mother and lamb in one day, must not seethe a kid in its mother's milk, must not muzzle the ox that treadeth out the corn.* The use, and the only use, of law is to prevent and punish for sin. All law has a penalty for those who violate it. Governments that are the greatest blessing to its citizens are those who can prohibit, or abolish the most sin or crime. Crime is not prevented by toleration, but by prohibition. Nine of the ten commandments are prohibitive and begin with, *Thou shalt not.*

The success of life, the formation of character, is in proportion to the courage one has to say to one's own self, *Thou shalt not.* It is not the man or woman who has no temptation to sin who has the strong character, but the man or woman who has the desire but will not yield to sin. Some people ask, why did God make the Devil? The Devil is God's fire. Like an alchemist, God is purifying souls. The Devil is an agent in salvation. Every Devil in hell is harnessed up to push every saint into heaven.

Those who are counted worthy to enter into the delights of that heavenly land are those who have had their *fiery trials*, tried and made white. Man would have no credit and could not hear, *Good and faithful servant,* if he had no temptations to do otherwise - man would be but a mere machine.

God has never used for his work any but those who prohibit evil. The Pilgrim Fathers were forced from the mother country because this principle of prohibition burned in their hearts. When England would oppose the colonies, it was prohibition that smashed the tea over in Boston Harbor. George Washington was put at the head of the colonial armies that prohibited, by much bloodshed and suffering, the oppression from the mother country. Our Civil War was the result of the principle to abolish or prohibit the slavery of the colored race. Now we have a worse slavery than England threatened us with or the poor blacks suffered at the hands of their taskmasters. This slavery of soul and body is one that leads to eternal death. The forces of darkness and death are with those who are willing to be led captive by the Devil at his will, and to lead others under this grievous yoke of those who are trying to perpetuate the cause of evil.

There are men who desire to be loyal, who are voting for license or in license parties, because they do not stop to think. The people are generally right on all questions. They go wrong more for lack of thought than for lack of heart. Edmund Burke, the greatest English statesman, said, *The people have as good government as they deserve.* Because the people have always had the power, and in America especially, they are sovereign. The President and all others in office are but servants of the people. . . .

Hear the language of the Declaration of Independence, *We hold these truths to be self-evident, that all men are created free and equal, that they are endowed by their Creator with certain inalienable rights, that among these are life, liberty, and the pursuit of happiness; that to secure these rights, governments are instituted among men deriving their just powers from the consent of the governed.* The licensing of intoxicating drink results in suicide and murder, whether or not the saloonkeeper or state be held responsible. Some one is. Who? The man who consents to or aids by his vote is most criminal. It is said that drink kills a man a minute. Suppose that we had a war that killed a man every five minutes. Would there not be howling for an end of bloodshed? This is more than ten times worse, for the soul is more valuable than the body.

Freedom or liberty in animals is following instinct and underlying appetite. Not so with man - to the reverse. It is the freedom of conscience and will from the bondage of ignorance of the person, the gratification of appetite and passion. The body is a good servant, but a tyrant when it is master. A man must be master or slave. One must first, like Daniel, *purpose in his heart that he will not defile himself.* Liberty or freedom is only attained by prohibition of opportunity to do wrong to ourselves or allow anyone else to do so. Citizenship not only requires one to obey law but must see that others do so also.

The principles of government are founded on liberty and self-control. Drunkenness is a loss of self-control. Anything that animalizes men is a menace to the life of the state and prevents the purpose of government. Thus, placing the weapon of destruction in the hands of its foes and the danger is great, because so many citizens are under the domination of their own will and passion. This class is being multiplied by this licensed crime. These willing classes are an integral part of the nation. By licensing rum, we are fostering a power that is increasing the weakness, and preventing the self-control, of its citizens. This is conspiracy, treason - black as night. Some plead the revenue of our wealth. Our wealth is in our citizens. The state cannot add to its treasury at the expense of its manhood without punishing herself. The state must guard the character of its citizens. It cannot make them honest, but it must punish dishonesty - cannot make them humane, but it must prohibit an act of inhumanity - and should oppose and forbid every license that man would desire or try to obtain that which would allow such gratification of the animal over the moral.

The nation is what its homes are. The family first, then the nation. Nothing can injure an individual or a family that is not an injury to the state. The fight for firesides means a fight for our national life. Our revolutionary sires fought for this. This is the fight that Carry A. Nation is making. It is the heart of love, liberty, and peace. Some of these thoughts I have copied from an article I read on a few leaves of a torn pamphlet, no name. But the writer has the true meaning of government. I am a prohibitionist because I am a Christian. I want to get to heaven. None but prohibitionists ever do. Hell is made for those who take license to sin.

Afterward
Carrie Nation died on June 9, 1911. Eight years later, the Eighteenth Amendment to the Constitution, National Prohibition, was enacted. It was repealed in 1933 by the Twenty-first Amendment.

Selected Reading

Asbury, Herbert, *Carry Nation*, 1929.

Beals, Carleton, *Cyclone Carrie*, 1962.

Madison, Arnold, *Carry Nation*, 1977.

Nation, Carry, *The Use and Need of the Life of Carry A. Nation*, 1905.

Taylor, Robert L., *Vessel of Wrath: The Life and Times of Carry Nation*, 1966.

Wilhoite, Lucy D., *The Hatchet Crusade: "Woman's Part in the Battle for Freedom"*, 1928.

Richard Nixon
Checkers
September 23, 1952

SECRET "MILLIONIARE'S CLUB" KEEPS NIXON IN LIFESTYLE FAR BEYOND HIS SALARY

The existence of a *millionaire's club* devoted to the financial comfort of Senator Richard Nixon, Republican Vice Presidential candidate, was revealed today.

- The New York Post, **September 18, 1952**

Long before the Watergate Scandal, Richard Nixon called *The Slush Fund Scandal "The most scarring personal crisis of my life."* He was selected by the 1952 Republican National Convention to be General Eisenhower's Vice Presidential running mate. The story of *The Slush Fund* - $18,235 given by local supporters - almost ruined him. The uproar over the Slush Fund (opponents called it bribe money) made Republican politicians call for Nixon's withdrawal or removal from the Republican Ticket. Nixon, unwilling to withdraw and afraid of being removed, bought for $75,000 30 minutes of television time to give his side of the story.

Richard Milhous Nixon was born on January 9, 1913 in Yorba Linda, California, the child of Frank and Hannah (Milhous) Nixon. Educated at Whittier College and Duke University Law School, he practiced law until his World War II service in the Navy. In 1946, running as a Republican, Nixon won election from California to the U.S. House of Representatives. Congressman Nixon, appointed to the House Un-American Activities Committee, gained a national reputation as a *red-hunter* in the Alger Hiss Spy Case. In 1950 he won election from California to the U.S. Senate. At the 1952 Republican National Convention, he was selected as the Vice Presidential candidate.

On September 23, 1952, appearing live on the NBC television network before an estimated audience of sixty million, Richard Nixon delivered this landmark speech, *Checkers.*

M_y fellow Americans, I come before you tonight as a candidate for the Vice Presidency and as a man whose honesty and integrity have been questioned. The usual political thing to do when charges are made against you is to either ignore them or to deny them without giving details.

I believe we've had enough of that in the United States, particularly with the present Administration in Washington, D.C. To me the office of the Vice Presidency of the United States is a great office, and I feel that the people have got to have confidence in the integrity of the men who run for that office and who might obtain it.

I have a theory, too, that the best and only answer to a smear or to an honest misunderstanding of the facts is to tell the truth. And that's why I'm here tonight. I want to tell you my side of the case.

I am sure that you have read the charge and you've heard that I, Senator Nixon, took $18,000 from a group of my supporters. . . . The question is, was it morally wrong? I say that it was morally wrong if any of that $18,000 went to Senator Nixon for my personal use. I say that it was morally wrong if it was secretly given and secretly handled. And I say that it was morally wrong if any of the contributors got special favors for the contributions that they made.

And now to answer those questions let me say this. . . . Not one cent of the $18,000 or any other money of that type ever went to me for my personal use. . . . It was not a secret fund. . . . And third, let me point out, and I want to make this particularly clear, that no contributor to this fund, no contributor to any of my campaign, has ever received any consideration that he would not have received as an ordinary constituent.

. . . . I realize that there are still some who may say, and rightly so, and let me say that I recognize that some will continue to smear regardless of what the truth may be, but that there has been understandably some honest misunderstanding on this matter, and there's some that will say. . . .

And so now what I am going to do, and incidentally this is unprecedented in the history of American politics, I am going at this time to give this television and radio audience a complete financial history, everything I've earned, everything I've spent, everything I owe.

. . . . Well, that's about it. That's what we have and that's what we owe. It isn't very much but Pat and I have the satisfaction that every dime we've got is honestly ours. I should say this - that Pat doesn't have a mink coat. But she does have a respectable Republican cloth coat. And I always tell her that she'd look good in anything.

One other thing I probably should tell you because if we don't they'll probably be saying this about me too, we did get something - a gift - after the election. A man down in Texas heard Pat on the radio mention the fact that our two youngsters would like to have a dog. And, believe it or not, the day before we left on this campaign trip we got a message from Union Station in Baltimore saying they had a package for us. We went down to get it. You know what it was.

It was a little cocker spaniel dog in a crate that he sent all the way from Texas. Black and white spotted. And our little girl - Tricia, the six-year-old - named it Checkers. And you know, the kids love the dog and I just want to say this right now, that regardless of what they say about it, we're gonna keep it.

. . . . Now, let me say this, I know that this is not the last of the smears. In spite of my explanation tonight other smears will be made; others have been made in the past. And the purpose of the smears, I know, is this, to silence me, to make me let up.

. . . . As far as this is concerned, I intend to continue the fight. . . . Why do I feel so deeply? Why do I feel that in spite of the smears, the misunderstandings, the necessities for a man to come up here and bare his soul as I have? Why is it necessary for me to continue this fight?

And I want to tell you why. Because, you see, I love my country. And I think my country is in danger. And I think that the only man who can save America at this time is the man that's running for President on my ticket - Dwight Eisenhower.

You say, *Why do I think it's in danger?* and I say look at the record. Seven years of the Truman Administration and what's happened? 600,000,000 people lost to the Communists, and a war in Korea in which we have lost 117,000 American casualties. And I say to all of you that a policy that results in a loss of 600,000,000 to the Communists and a war which costs us 117,000 American casualties isn't good enough for America. And I say that those in the State Department that made the mistakes which caused that war and which resulted in those losses should be kicked out of the State Department just as fast as we can get 'em out of there.

. . . . And I say that the only man who can lead us in this fight to rid the Government of both those who are Communists and those who have corrupted this Government is Eisenhower, because Eisenhower, you can be sure, recognizes the problem and he knows how to deal with it.

And, now, finally, I know that you wonder whether or not I am going to stay on the Republican ticket or resign. Let me say this, I don't believe that I ought to quit because I'm not a quitter. . . .

But the decision, my friends, is not mine. I would do nothing that would harm the possibilities of Dwight Eisenhower to become President of the United States. And for that reason I am submitting to the Republican National Committee tonight through this television broadcast the decision which it is theirs to make. Let them decide whether my position on the ticket will help or hurt. And I am going to ask you to help them decide. Wire and write the Republican National Committee whether you think I should stay on or whether I should get off. And whatever their decision is, I will abide by it.

But just let me say this last word. Regardless of what happens I'm going to continue this fight. I'm going to campaign up and down America until we drive the crooks and the Communists and those that defend them out of Washington. And remember, folks, Eisenhower is a great man. Believe me. He's a great man. And a vote for Eisenhower is a vote for what's good for America.

Afterward

The *Checkers Speech* kept Richard Nixon on the winning 1952 Republican Ticket. Nixon went on to run for President three times. He lost in 1960, won in 1968, and in 1972 won re-election. He was forced to resign, for his part in the Watergate Scandal, on August 9, 1974.

Richard Nixon died on April 22, 1994.

Selected Reading

Aitken, Jonathan, *Nixon: A Life*, 1993.

Ambrose, Stephen, *Nixon*, 1987.

Crowley, Monica, *Nixon in Winter*, 1998.

de Toledano, Ralph, *One Man Alone: Richard Nixon*, 1969.

Johnson, George, *Richard Nixon*, 1961.

Kissinger, Henry, *Years of Upheaval*, 1982.

Kornitzer, Bela, *The Real Nixon: An Intimate Biography*, 1960.

Mankiewicz, Frank, *Perfectly Clear: Nixon from Whittier to Watergate*, 1973.

Mazo, Earl, *Richard Nixon*, 1960.

Morris, Roger, *Richard Milhous Nixon*, 1990.

Nixon, Richard M., *RN: The Memoirs of Richard Nixon*, 1990.

Woodward, Bob, *The Final Days*, 1977.

Colin Powell
Sharing The American Dream
April 28, 1997

Our strategy for going after the Iraqi Army in Kuwait is very simple. First we are going to cut it off, and then we are going to kill it.
- General Colin Powell, January 17, 1991

In August 1990 Iraq invaded Kuwait. Once the decision to liberate Kuwait was made, the military strategy to carry out that decision fell to the first African American Chairman of the Joint Chiefs of Staff, General Colin Powell.

Colin Luther Powell was born on April 5, 1937 in New York City, the child of Jamaican immigrants Luther and Maud (McKoy) Powell. Educated at New York's City College, Powell entered the U.S. Army. Serving two tours of duty in Vietnam (1962-63, and 1968-69), Colin Powell won the Purple Heart, the Bronze Star, the Soldier's Medal, and the Legion of Merit. Rising in the ranks, he went on to lead the 101st Airborne Division, the Fourth Infantry Division, and the Fifth Corps. Powell, having attained the rank of General, served as Military Assistant to the Secretary of Defense (1983-86), as the President's National Security Advisor (1987-89), and as Chairman of the Joint Chiefs of Staff (1989-93). In this capacity, he oversaw Operation Desert Storm - The Gulf War.

After thirty-five years in the military, General Powell retired in 1993. As a private citizen, he became involved in the humanitarian effort to aid, through volunteerism, the more than 2 million American children living in poverty.

On April 28, 1997, from the steps of Philadelphia's Independence Hall, Colin Powell - after telling an interviewer, *I have arrived at a point in my life where I am trying to use what I have been given by my nation to help my nation* - delivered this landmark address on the need for American volunteerism, *Sharing The American Dream.*

Over 200 years ago a group of volunteers gathered on this sacred spot to found a new nation. In perfect words, they voiced their dreams and aspirations of an imperfect world. They pledged their lives, their fortune and their sacred honor to secure inalienable rights given by God for life, liberty and pursuit of happiness, pledged that they would provide them to all who would inhabit this new nation.

They look down on us today in spirit, with pride for all we have done to keep faith with their ideals and their sacrifices. Yet, despite all we have done this is still an imperfect world. We still live in an imperfect society. Despite more than two centuries of moral and material progress, despite all our efforts to achieve a more perfect union, there are still Americans who are not sharing in the American Dream. There are still Americans who wonder is the journey there for them, is the dream there for them, or whether it is, at best, a dream deferred.

The great American poet, Langston Hughes, talked about a dream deferred, and he said,

> *What happens to a dream deferred? Does it dry up like a raisin in the sun, or fester like a sore and then run? Does it stink like rotten meat or crust and sugar over like a syrupy sweet? Maybe it just sags, like a heavy load. Or, does it explode?*

For too many young Americans, that dream deferred does sag like a heavy load that's pushing them down into the ground, and they wonder if they can rise up with that load. And as we see too often in our daily life, it does explode in violence, in youngsters falling dead, shot by other youngsters. It does explode, and it has the potential to explode our society.

So today, we gather here today to pledge that the dream must no longer be deferred and it will never, as long as we can do anything about it, become a dream denied. That is why we are here, my friends. We gather here to pledge that those of us who are more fortunate will not forsake those who are less fortunate. We are a compassionate and caring people. We are a generous people. We will reach down, we will reach back, we will reach across to help our brothers and sisters who are in need.

Above all, we pledge to reach out to the most vulnerable members of the American family, our children. As you've heard, up to 15 million young Americans today are at risk. They are at risk of growing up unskilled, unlearned or, even worse, unloved. They are at risk of growing up physically or psychologically abused. They are at risk of growing up addicted to the pathologies and poisons of the street. They are at risk of bringing up children into the world before they themselves have grown up. They are at risk of never growing up at all. Fifteen million young lives are at risk, may not make it unless we care enough to do something about it.

In terms of numbers the task may seem staggering. But if we look at the simple needs that these children have, then the task is manageable. The goal is achievable. We know what they need. They need an adult caring person in their life, a safe place to learn and grow, a healthy start, marketable skills and an opportunity to serve so that early in their lives they learn the virtue of service so that they can reach out then and touch another young American in need.

These are basic needs that we commit ourselves today, we promise today. We are making America's promise today to provide to those children in need. This is a grand alliance. It is an alliance between government and corporate America and nonprofit America, between our institutions of faith, but especially between individual Americans.

You heard the governors and the mayors, and you'll hear more in a little minute that says the real answer is for each and every one of us, not just here in Philadelphia, but across this land, for each and every one of us to reach out and touch someone in need. All of us can spare 30 minutes a week or an hour a week. All of us can give an extra dollar. All of us can touch someone who doesn't look like us, who doesn't speak like us, who may not dress like us, but, by God, needs us in their lives. And that's what we all have to do to keep this going. And so there's a spirit of Philadelphia here today. There's a spirit of Philadelphia that we saw yesterday in Germantown. There is a spirit of Philadelphia that will leave Philadelphia tomorrow afternoon and spread across this whole nation - 30 governors will go back and spread it; over 100 mayors will go back and spread it, and hundreds of others, leaders around this country who are watching, will go back and spread it. Corporate America will spread it. Non-profits will spread it. And each and every one of us will spread it because it has to be done, we have no choice. We cannot leave these children behind if we are going to meet the dreams of our founding fathers.

And so let us all join in this great crusade. Let us make sure that no child in America is left behind, no child in America has their dream deferred or denied. We can do it. We can do it because we are Americans. We are Americans who draw our strength from this place. We are Americans who believe to the depth of our hearts that this is not a land that was put here by historic accident, it is a land that was put here by Divine Providence, who told us to be good stewards of the land, but especially to be good stewards of each other. Divine Providence gave us this land, blessed it and told us always to be proud to call it America.

And so we go forward. Let's go save our children.

Afterward

Colin Powell's efforts to motivate and organize volunteers continues today. In his 1993 biography, *My American Journey*, he wrote, *As one who has received so much from his country, I feel a heavy debt, and I can never be entirely free of it. My responsibility, our responsibility as lucky Americans, is to try to give back to this country as much as it has given to us.*

Selected Reading

Means, Howard B., *Colin Powell: Soldier/Statesman*, 1992.
Powell, Colin L., *My American Journey*, 1995.
Roth, David, *Sacred Honor: A Biography of Colin Powell*, 1993.
Shaw, Lisa, Editor, *In His Own Words: Colin Powell*, 1995.

Ronald Reagan
The Reagan Revolution
January 20, 1981

It's time we asked ourselves if we still know the freedoms intended for us by the Founding Fathers. James Madison said, "We base all our experiments on the capacity of mankind for self-government." This idea that government was beholden to the people, that it had no other source of power, is still the newest, most unique idea in all the long history of man's relation to man. This is the issue of this election - whether we believe in our capacity for self-government or whether we abandon the American Revolution and confess that a little intellectual elite in a far-distant capital can plan our lives for us better than we can plan them ourselves.

- Ronald Reagan, *A Time For Choosing,* 1964

Ronald Reagan, who believed *the ills of this nation stem from a single source - the mistaken belief that government, particularly the Federal Government, has the answer to our ills,* delivered his first *"Government is not the solution to our problems - government is the problem"* speech during the 1964 Presidential election. Nearly sixteen years later, Ronald Reagan, in accepting the Republican Party's 1980 Presidential nomination, was still expounding this theme - *We are going to put an end to the notion that the American taxpayer exists to fund the federal Government.*

Ronald Wilson Reagan, *The Great Communicator,* was born on February 6, 1911 in Tampico, Illinois, the child of John and Nelle (Wilson) Reagan. Educated at Peoria, Illinois' Eureka College, Reagan worked as a sportscaster (1932-37), a Hollywood actor (1937-46), and a corporate spokesperson (1954-65). Entering politics, he was twice elected and served as Governor of California (1967-74), and in 1980 he was elected, in a landslide, President of the United States.

On January 20, 1981, at the U.S. Capitol in Washington, D.C., Ronald Reagan began his Presidency by delivering this landmark Inaugural Address, *The Reagan Revolution.*

My fellow citizens, to a few of us here today this is a solemn and most momentous occasion, and yet in the history of our nation it is a commonplace occurrence. The orderly transfer of authority as called for in the Constitution routinely takes place, as it has for almost two centuries, and few of us stop to think how unique we really are. In the eyes of many in the world, this every-four-year ceremony we accept as normal is nothing less than a miracle.

Mr. President, I want our fellow citizens to know how much you did to carry on this tradition. By your gracious cooperation in the transition process, you have shown a watching world that we are a united people pledged to maintaining a political system which guarantees individual liberty to a greater degree than any other, and I thank you and your people for all your help in maintaining the continuity which is the bulwark of our Republic.

The business of our nation goes forward. These United States are confronted with an economic affliction of great proportions. We suffer from the longest and one of the worst sustained inflations in our national history. It distorts our economic decisions, penalizes thrift, and crushes the struggling young and the fixed-income elderly alike. It threatens to shatter the lives of millions of our people.

Idle industries have cast workers into unemployment, human misery, and personal indignity. Those who do work are denied a fair return for their labor by a tax system which penalizes successful achievement and keeps us from maintaining full productivity.

But great as our tax burden is, it has not kept pace with public spending. For decades we have piled deficit upon deficit, mortgaging our future and our children's future for the temporary convenience of the present. To continue this long trend is to guarantee tremendous social, cultural, political, and economic upheavals.

You and I, as individuals, can, by borrowing, live beyond our means, but for only a limited period of time. Why, then, should we think that collectively, as a nation, we're not bound by that same limitation? We must act today in order to preserve tomorrow. And let there be no misunderstanding - we are going to begin to act, beginning today.

The economic ills we suffer have come upon us over several decades. They will not go away in days, weeks, or months, but they will go away. They will go away because we as Americans have the capacity now, as we've had in the past, to do whatever needs to be done to preserve this last and greatest bastion of freedom.

In this present crisis, government is not the solution to our problem - government is the problem. From time to time we've been tempted to believe that society has become too complex to be managed by self-rule, that government by an elite group is superior to government for, by, and of the people. Well, if no one among us is capable of governing himself, then who among us has the capacity to govern someone else? All of us together, in and out of government, must bear the burden. The solutions we seek must be equitable, with no one group singled out to pay a higher price.

We hear much of special interest groups. Well, our concern must be for a special interest group that has been too long neglected. It knows no sectional boundaries or ethnic and racial divisions, and it crosses political party lines. It is made up of men and women who raise our food, patrol our streets, man our mines and factories, teach our children, keep our homes, and heal us when we're sick - professionals, industrialists, shopkeepers, clerks, cabbies, and truck drivers. They are, in short, *We the people*, this breed called Americans.

Well, this administration's objective will be a healthy, vigorous, growing economy that provides equal opportunities for all Americans, with no barriers born of bigotry or discrimination. Putting America back to work means putting all Americans back to work. Ending inflation means freeing all Americans from the terror of runaway living costs. All must share in the productive work of this *new beginning*, and all must share in the bounty of a revived economy. With the idealism and fair play which are the core of our system and our strength, we can have a strong and prosperous America, at peace with itself and the world.

So, as we begin, let us take inventory. We are a nation that has a government - not the other way around. And this makes us special among the nations of the Earth. Our government has no power except that granted it by the people. It is time to check and reverse the growth of government, which shows signs of having grown beyond the consent of the governed.

It is my intention to curb the size and influence of the Federal establishment and to demand recognition of the distinction between the powers granted to the Federal Government and those reserved to the States or to the people. All of us need to be reminded that the Federal Government did not create the States - the States created the Federal Government.

Now, so there will be no misunderstanding - it's not my intention to do away with government. It is rather to make it work - work with us, not over us - to stand by our side, not ride on our back. Government can and must provide opportunity, not smother it - foster productivity, not stifle it.

If we look to the answer as to why for so many years we achieved so much, prospered as no other people on Earth, it was because here in this land we unleashed the energy and individual genius of man to a greater extent than has ever been done before. Freedom and the dignity of the individual have been more available and assured here than in any other place on Earth. The price for this freedom at times has been high, but we have never been unwilling to pay that price.

It is no coincidence that our present troubles parallel and are proportionate to the intervention and intrusion in our lives that result from unnecessary and excessive growth of government. It is time for us to realize that we're too great a nation to limit ourselves to small dreams. We're not, as some would have us believe, doomed to an inevitable decline. I do not believe in a fate that will fall on us no matter what we do. I do believe in a fate that will fall on us if we do nothing. So, with all the creative energy at our command, let us begin an era of national renewal. Let us renew our determination, our courage, and our strength. And let us renew our faith and our hope.

We have every right to dream heroic dreams. Those who say that we're in a time when there are not heroes - they just don't know where to look. You can see heroes every day going in and out of factory gates. Others, a handful in number, produce enough food to feed all of us and then the world beyond. You meet heroes across a counter, and they're on both sides of that counter. There are entrepreneurs with faith in themselves, and faith in an idea, who create new jobs, new wealth, and opportunity. They're individuals and families whose taxes support the government and whose voluntary gifts support church, charity, culture, art, and education. Their patriotism is quiet but deep. Their values sustain our national life.

Now, I have used the words *they* and *their* in speaking of these heroes. I could say *you* and *your,* because I'm addressing the heroes of whom I speak - you, the citizens of this blessed land. Your dreams, your hopes, your goals are going to be the dreams, the hopes, and the goals of this administration, so help me God.

We shall reflect the compassion that is so much a part of your makeup. How can we love our country and not love our countrymen - and loving them, reach out a hand when they fall, heal them when they're sick, and provide opportunity to make them self-sufficient so they will be equal in fact and not just in theory?

Can we solve the problems confronting us? Well, the answer is an unequivocal and emphatic *yes.* To paraphrase Winston Churchill, I did not take the oath I've just taken with the intention of presiding over the dissolution of the world's strongest economy.

In the days ahead I will propose removing the roadblocks that have slowed our economy and reduced productivity. Steps will be taken aimed at restoring the balance between the various levels of government. Progress may be slow, measured in inches and feet, not miles, but we will progress. It is time to reawaken this industrial giant, to get government back within its means, and to lighten our punitive tax burden. And these will be our first priorities, and on these principles there will be no compromise.

On the eve of our struggle for independence a man who might have been one of the greatest among the Founding Fathers, Dr. Joseph Warren, president of the Massachusetts Congress, said to his fellow Americans,

Our country is in danger, but not to be despaired of. . . . On you depend the fortunes of America. You are to decide the important questions upon which rests the happiness and the liberty of millions yet unborn. Act worthy of yourselves.

Well, I believe we, the Americans of today, are ready to act worthy of ourselves, ready to do what must be done to ensure happiness and liberty for ourselves, our children, and our children's children. And, as we renew ourselves here in our own land, we will be seen as having greater strength throughout the world. We will again be the exemplar of freedom and a beacon of hope for those who do not now have freedom.

To those neighbors and allies who share our freedom, we will strengthen our historic ties and assure them of our support and firm commitment. We will match loyalty with loyalty. We will strive for mutually beneficial relations. We will not use our friendship to impose on their sovereignty, for our own sovereignty is not for sale.

As for the enemies of freedom, those who are potential adversaries, they will be reminded that peace is the highest aspiration of the American people. We will negotiate for it, sacrifice for it; we will not surrender for it, now or ever.

Our forbearance should never be misunderstood. Our reluctance for conflict should not be misjudged as a failure of will. When action is required to preserve our national security, we will act. We will maintain sufficient strength to prevail if need be, knowing that if we do so we have the best chance of never having to use that strength.

Above all, we must realize that no arsenal or no weapon in the arsenals of the world is so formidable as the will and moral courage of free men and women. It is a weapon our adversaries in today's world do not have. It is a weapon that we as Americans do have. Let that be understood by those who practice terrorism and prey upon their neighbors.

I'm told that tens of thousands of prayer meetings are being held on this day, and for that I'm deeply grateful. We are a nation under God, and I believe God intended for us to be free. It would be fitting and good, I think, if on each Inaugural Day in future years it should be declared a day of prayer.

This is the first time in our history that this ceremony has been held, as you've been told, on this West Front of the Capitol. Standing here, one faces a magnificent vista, opening up on this city's special beauty and history. At the end of this open mall are those shrines to the giants on whose shoulders we stand.

Directly in front of me, the monument to a monumental man, George Washington, father of our country. A man of humility who came to greatness reluctantly. He led America out of revolutionary victory into infant nationhood. Off to one side, the stately memorial to Thomas Jefferson. The Declaration of Independence flames with his eloquence. And then, beyond the Reflecting Pool, the dignified columns of the Lincoln Memorial. Whoever would understand in his heart the meaning of America will find it in the life of Abraham Lincoln.

Beyond those monuments to heroism is the Potomac River, and on the far shore the sloping hills of Arlington National Cemetery, with its row upon row of simple white markers bearing crosses or Stars of David. They add up to only a tiny fraction of the price that has been paid for our freedom.

Each one of those markers is a monument to the kind of hero I spoke of earlier. Their lives ended in places called

Belleau Wood, The Argonne, Omaha Beach, Salerno, and halfway around the world on Guadalcanal, Tarawa, Pork Chop Hill, and Chosin Reservoir, and in a hundred rice paddies and jungles of a place called Vietnam.

Under one such marker lies a young man, Martin Treptow, who left his job in a small town barbershop in 1917 to go to France with the famed Rainbow Division. There, on the western front, he was killed trying to carry a message between battalions under heavy artillery fire. We're told that on his body was found a diary. On the flyleaf under the heading, *My Pledge*, he had written these words,

> *America must win this war. Therefore I will work, I will save, I will sacrifice, I will endure, I will fight cheerfully and do my utmost, as if the issue of the whole struggle depended on me alone.*

The crisis we are facing today does not require of us the kind of sacrifice that Martin Treptow and so many thousands of others were called upon to make. It does require, however, our best effort and our willingness to believe in ourselves and to believe in our capacity to perform great deeds, to believe that together with God's help we can and will resolve the problems which now confront us.

And, after all, why shouldn't we believe that? We are Americans.

God bless you, and thank you.

Ronald Reagan

Afterward

Ronald Reagan served two terms as President. In 1984 he summed up his feelings about America, *The poet called Miss Liberty's torch, "the lamp beside the golden door." Well, that was the entrance to America, and it still is. The glistening hope of that lamp is still ours. Every promise, every opportunity, is still golden in this land. And through that golden door our children can walk into tomorrow with the knowledge that no one can be denied the promise that is America. Her heart is full; her torch is still golden, her future bright. She has arms big enough to comfort and strong enough to support, for the strength in her arms is the strength of her people. She will carry on unafraid, unashamed, and unsurpassed. In this springtime of hope, some lights seem eternal; America's is.*

Selected Reading

Anderson, Martin, *Revolution: The Reagan Legacy*, 1990.

Berman, Larry, Editor, *Looking Back on the Reagan Presidency*, 1990.

Blumenthal, Sidney, and Thomas Byrne Edsall, Editors, *The Reagan Legacy*, 1988.

Cannon, Lou, *Reagan*, 1982.

D'Souza, Dinesh, *Ronald Reagan*, 1997.

Hannaford, Peter, *The Reagans: A Political Portrait*, 1983.

Reagan, Maureen, *First Father, First Daughter*, 1989.

Reagan, Michael, with Jim Denney, *The City on a Hill: Fulfilling Ronald Reagan's Vision for America*, 1997.

Reagan, Ronald, *An American Life*, 1990.

Speakes, Larry, with Robert Pack, *Speaking Out*, 1988.

Wills, Garry, *Reagan's America*, 1988.

Eleanor Roosevelt
Human Rights
September 28, 1948

When you cease to make a contribution, you die.

- Eleanor Roosevelt

Anna Eleanor Roosevelt, who spent her life making a contribution, was born on October 11, 1884 in New York City, the child of Elliott and Anna (Hill) Roosevelt. After the death of her parents (her mother when she was eight, her father when she was ten), Eleanor was raised by her maternal grandmother. Educated at London's Allenswood School, she returned to New York City at the age of eighteen. She married her cousin Franklin in 1905 and, between 1906 and 1916, had five children. While Franklin Delano Roosevelt (see page 158) pursued his political career, Eleanor, believing that *women must learn to play the game as men do,* pursued two controversial activist careers - a feminist career, working for women's rights legislation with the League of Women Voters - and, believing *government has a responsibility to defend the weak,* a social reform career, working for civil rights legislation with the NAACP. As First Lady of the United States (1934-45), Eleanor Roosevelt was instrumental in fashioning into the New Deal her own feminist and social reform agendas.

In April 1945 Eleanor Roosevelt, then sixty years old, became a widow. In 1946 the former First Lady was appointed by President Truman as a delegate to the United Nations General Assembly. The General Assembly appointed her Chairwoman of the Human Rights Commission, with the mission of drafting *A Universal Declaration of Human Rights - a Bill of Rights for the World.*

On September 28, 1948, speaking at the Sorbonne University in Paris, Eleanor Roosevelt, in an effort to win General Assembly passage of the proposed Declaration, delivered this landmark speech, *Human Rights.*

I have come this evening to talk with you on one of the greatest issues of our time, that is, the preservation of human freedom. I have chosen to discuss it here in France, at the Sorbonne, because here in this soil the roots of human freedom have long ago struck deep and here they have been richly nourished. It was here the Declaration of the Rights of Man was proclaimed, and the great slogans of the French Revolution - liberty, equality, fraternity - fired the imagination of men. I have chosen to discuss this issue in Europe because this has been the scene of the greatest historic battles between freedom and tyranny. I have chosen to discuss it in the early days of the General Assembly because the issue of human liberty is decisive for the settlement of outstanding political differences and for the future of the United Nations.

The decisive importance of this issue was fully recognized by the founders of the United Nations at San Francisco. Concern for the preservation and promotion of human rights and fundamental freedoms stands at the heart of the United Nations. Its Charter is distinguished by its preoccupation with the rights and welfare of individual men and women. The United Nations has made it clear that it intends to uphold human rights and to protect the dignity of the human personality. In the preamble to the Charter the keynote is set when it declares, *We the people of the United Nations determined . . . to reaffirm faith in fundamental human rights, in the dignity and worth of the human person, in the equal rights of men and women and of nations large and small, and . . . to promote social progress and better standards of life in larger freedom.* This reflects the basic premise of the Charter that the peace and security of mankind are dependent on mutual respect for the rights and freedoms of all.

One of the purposes of the United Nations is declared in Article One to be *to achieve international cooperation in solving international problems of an economic, social, cultural, or humanitarian character, and in promoting and encouraging respect for human rights and for fundamental freedoms for all without distinction as to race, sex, language, or religion.*

. . . . The Human Rights Commission was given as its first and most important task the preparation of an International Bill of Rights. The General Assembly which opened its third session here in Paris a few days ago will have before it the first fruit of the Commission's labors in this task, that is, the International Declaration of Human Rights. This Declaration was finally completed after much work during the last session of the Human Rights Commission in New York in the spring of 1948. The Economic and Social Council has sent it without recommendation to the General Assembly, together with other documents transmitted by the Human Rights Commission.

It was decided in our Commission that a Bill of Rights should contain two parts:

One. A Declaration which could be approved through action of the Member States of the United Nations in the General Assembly. This Declaration would have great moral force and would say to the peoples of the world, *this is what we hope human rights may mean to all people in the years to come.* We have put down here the rights that we consider basic for individual human beings the world over to have. Without them, we feel that the full development of individual personality is impossible.

Two. The second part of the bill, which the Human Rights Commission has not yet completed because of the lack of time, is a covenant which would be in the form of a treaty to be presented to the nations of the world. Each nation, as it is prepared to do so, would ratify this covenant and the covenant would then become binding on the nations which adhere to it. Each nation ratifying would then be obligated to change its laws wherever they did not conform to the points contained in the covenant.

This covenant, of course, would have to be a simpler document. It could not state aspirations, which we feel to be permissible in the Declaration. It could only state rights which could be assured by law and it must contain methods of implementation, and no state ratifying the covenant could be allowed to disregard it. The methods of implementation have not yet been agreed upon, nor have they been given adequate consideration by the Commission at any of its meetings. There certainly should be discussion on the entire question of this world Bill of Human Rights and there may be acceptance by this Assembly of the Declaration if they come to agreement on it. The acceptance of the Declaration, I think, should encourage every nation in the coming months to discuss its meaning with its people so that they will be better prepared to accept the covenant with a deeper understanding of the problems involved when that is presented, we hope, a year from now and, we hope, accepted.

The Declaration has come from the Human Rights Commission with unanimous acceptance except for four abstentions - the U.S.S.R., Yugoslavia, Ukraine, and Byelorussia. The reason for this is a fundamental difference in the conception of human rights as they exist in these states and in certain other Member States in the United Nations.

In the discussion before the Assembly, I think it should be made crystal clear what these differences are and tonight I want to spend a little time making them clear to you. It seems to me there is a valid reason for taking the time today to think carefully and clearly on the subject of human rights, because in the acceptance and observance of these rights lies the root, I believe, of our chance for peace in the future, and for the strengthening of the United Nations organization to the point where it can maintain peace in the future.

We must not be confused about what freedom is. Basic human rights are simple and easily understood - freedom of speech and a free press - freedom of religion and worship - freedom of assembly and the right of petition - the right of men to be secure in their homes and free from unreasonable search and seizure and from arbitrary arrest and punishment.

We must not be deluded by the efforts of the forces of reaction to prostitute the great words of our free tradition and thereby to confuse the struggle. Democracy, freedom, human rights have come to have a definite meaning to the people of the world which we must not allow any nation to so change that they are made synonymous with suppression and dictatorship.

There are basic differences that show up even in the use of words between a democratic and a totalitarian country. For instance, *democracy* means one thing to the U.S.S.R. and another to the U.S.A. and, I know, in France. I have served since the first meeting of the nuclear commission on the Human Rights Commission, and I think this point stands out clearly.

The U.S.S.R. Representatives assert that they already have achieved many things which we, in what they call the *bourgeois democracies*, cannot achieve because their government controls the accomplishment of these things. Our government seems powerless to them because, in the last analysis, it is controlled by the people. They would not put it that way - they would say that the people in the U.S.S.R. control their government by allowing their government to have certain absolute rights. We, on the other hand, feel that certain rights can never be granted to the government, but must be kept in the hands of the people.

For instance, the U.S.S.R. will assert that their press is free because the state makes it free by providing the machinery, the paper, and even the money for salaries for the people who work on the paper. They state that there is no control over what is printed in the various papers that they subsidize in this manner, such, for instance, as a trade union paper. But what would happen if a paper were to print ideas which were critical of the basic policies and beliefs of the Communist government? I am sure some good reason would be found for abolishing the paper.

It is true that there have been many cases where newspapers in the U.S.S.R. have criticized officials and their actions and have been responsible for the removal of those officials, but in doing so they did not criticize anything which was fundamental to Communist beliefs. They simply criticized methods of doing things, so one must differentiate between things which are permissible, such as criticism of any individual or of the manner of doing things, and the criticism of a belief which would be considered vital to the acceptance of Communism.

. . . . We, in the democracies, believe in a kind of international respect and action which is reciprocal. We do not think others should treat us differently from the way they wish to be treated. It is interference in other countries that especially stirs up antagonism against the Soviet Government. If it wishes to feel secure in developing its economic and political theories within its territory, then it should grant to others that same security. We believe in the freedom of people to make their own mistakes. We do not interfere with them and they should not interfere with others.

The basic problem confronting the world today, as I said in the beginning, is the preservation of human freedom for the individual and consequently for the society of which he is a part. We are fighting this battle again today as it was fought at the time of the French Revolution and at the time of the American Revolution. The issue of human liberty is as decisive now as it was then. I want to give you my conception of what is meant in my country by freedom of the individual.

Long ago in London during a discussion with Mr. Vyshinsky, he told me there was no such thing as freedom for the individual in the world. All freedom of the individual was conditioned by the rights of other individuals. That, of course, I granted. I said, *We approach the question from a different point of view; we here in the United Nations are trying to develop ideals which will be broader in outlook, which will consider first the rights of man, which will consider what makes man more free - not governments, but man.* The totalitarian state typically places the will of the people second to decrees promulgated by a few men at the top.

Naturally there must always be consideration of the rights of others; but in a democracy this is not a restriction. Indeed, in our democracies we make our freedoms secure because each of us is expected to respect the rights of others and we are free to make our own laws.

Freedom for our peoples is not only a right, but also a tool. Freedom of speech, freedom of the press, freedom of in formation, freedom of assembly - these are not just abstract ideals to us; they are tools with which we create a way of life, a way of life in which we can enjoy freedom.

Sometimes the processes of democracy are slow, and I have known some of our leaders to say that a benevolent dictatorship would accomplish the ends desired in a much shorter time than it takes to go through the democratic processes of discussion and the slow formation of public opinion. But there is no way of insuring that a dictatorship will remain benevolent or that power once in the hands of a few will be returned to the people without struggle or revolution. This we have learned by experience and we accept the slow processes of democracy because we know that shortcuts compromise principles on which no compromise is possible.

The final expression of the opinion of the people with us is through free and honest elections, with valid choices on basic issues and candidates. The secret ballot is an essential to free elections but you must have a choice before you. I have heard my husband say many times that a people need never lose their freedom if they kept their right to a secret ballot and if they used that secret ballot to the full.

Basic decisions of our society are made through the expressed will of the people. That is why when we see these liberties threatened, instead of falling apart, our nation becomes unified and our democracies come together as a unified group in spite of our varied backgrounds and many racial strains.

In the United States we have a capitalistic economy. That is because public opinion favors that type of economy under the conditions in which we live. But we have imposed certain restraints; for instance, we have antitrust laws. These are the legal evidence of the determination of the American people to maintain an economy of free competition and not to allow monopolies to take away the people's freedom.

Our trade unions grow stronger because the people come to believe that this is the proper way to guarantee the rights of the workers and that the right to organize and to bargain collectively keeps the balance between the actual producer and the investor of money and the manager in industry who watches over the man who works with his hands and who produces the materials which are our tangible wealth.

In the United States we are old enough not to claim perfection. We recognize that we have some problems of discrimination but we find steady progress being made in the solution of these problems. Through normal democratic processes we are coming to understand our needs and how we can attain full equality for all our people. Free discussion on the subject is permitted. Our Supreme Court has recently rendered decisions to clarify a number of our laws to guarantee the rights of all.

The U.S.S.R. claims it has reached a point where all races within her borders are officially considered equal and have equal rights and they insist they have no discrimination where minorities are concerned. This is a laudable objective but there are other aspects of the development of freedom for the individual which are essential before the mere absence of discrimination is worth much, and these are lacking in the Soviet Union. Unless they are being denied freedoms which they want and which they see other people have, people do not usually complain of discrimination. It is these other freedoms - the basic freedoms of speech, of the press, of religion and conscience, of assembly, of fair trial and freedom from arbitrary arrest and punishment -

which a totalitarian government cannot safely give its people and which give meaning to freedom from discrimination. It is my belief, and I am sure it is also yours, that the struggle for democracy and freedom is a critical struggle, for their preservation is essential to the great objective of the United Nations to maintain international peace and security.

Among free men the end cannot justify the means. We know the patterns of totalitarianism - the single political party, the control of schools, press, radio, the arts, the sciences, and the church to support autocratic authority; these are the age-old patterns against which men have struggled for three thousand years. These are the signs of reaction, retreat, and retrogression.

The United Nations must hold fast to the heritage of freedom won by the struggle of its peoples; it must help us to pass it on to generations to come. The development of the ideal of freedom and its translation into the everyday life of the people in great areas of the earth is the product of the efforts of many peoples. It is the fruit of a long tradition of vigorous thinking and courageous action. No one race and no one people can claim to have done all the work to achieve greater dignity for human beings and greater freedom to develop human personality. In each generation and in each country there must be a continuation of the struggle and new steps forward must be taken since this is pre-eminently a field in which to stand still is to retreat.

The field of human rights is not one in which compromise on fundamental principles are possible. The work of the Commission on Human Rights is illustrative. The Declaration of Human Rights provides, *Everyone has the right to leave any country, including his own.* The Soviet Representative said he would agree to this right if a single phrase was added to it - *in accordance with the procedure laid down in the laws of that country.* It is obvious that to accept this would be not only to compromise but to nullify the right stated. This case forcefully illustrates the importance of the proposition that we must ever be alert not to compromise fundamental human rights merely for the sake of reaching unanimity and thus lose them.

As I see it, it is not going to be easy to attain unanimity with respect to our different concepts of government and human rights. The struggle is bound to be difficult and one in which we must be firm but patient. If we adhere faithfully to our principles, I think it is possible for us to maintain freedom and to do so peacefully and without recourse to force.

The future must see the broadening of human rights throughout the world. People who have glimpsed freedom will never be content until they have secured it for themselves. In a true sense, human rights are a fundamental object of law and government in a just society. Human rights exist to the degree that they are respected by people in relations with each other and by governments in relations with their citizens.

The world at large is aware of the tragic consequences for human beings ruled by totalitarian systems. If we examine Hitler's rise to power, we see how the chains are forged which keep the individual a slave and we can see many similarities in the way things are accomplished in other countries. Politically men must be free to discuss and to arrive at as many facts as possible and there must be at least a two-party system in a country because when there is only one political party, too many things can be subordinated to the interests of that one party and it becomes a tyrant and not an instrument of democratic government.

The propaganda we have witnessed in the recent past, like that we perceive in these days, seeks to impugn, to undermine, and to destroy the liberty and independence of peoples. Such propaganda poses to all peoples the issue whether to doubt their heritage of rights and therefore to compromise the principles by which they live, or try to accept the challenge, redouble their vigilance, and stand steadfast in the struggle to maintain and enlarge human freedoms.

People who continue to be denied the respect to which they are entitled as human beings will not acquiesce forever in such denial.

The Charter of the United Nations is a guiding beacon along the way to the achievement of human rights and fundamental freedoms throughout the world. The immediate test is not only the extent to which human rights and freedoms have already been achieved, but the direction in which the world is moving. Is there a faithful compliance with the objectives of the Charter if some countries continue to curtail human rights and freedoms instead of to promote the universal respect for an observance of human rights and freedoms for all as called for by the Charter?

The place to discuss the issue of human rights is in the forum of the United Nations. The United Nations has been set up as the common meeting ground for nations, where we can consider together our mutual problems and take advantage of our differences in experience. It is inherent in our firm attachment to democracy and freedom that we stand always ready to use the fundamental democratic procedures of honest discussion and negotiation. It is now, as always, our hope that despite the wide differences in approach we face in the world today, we can, with mutual good faith in the principles of the United Nations Charter, arrive at a common basis of understanding.

We are here to join the meetings of this great international Assembly which meets in your beautiful capital city of Paris. Freedom for the individual is an inseparable part of the cherished traditions of France. As one of the Delegates from the United States, I pray Almighty God that we may win another victory here for the rights and freedoms of all men.

Afterward

On December 10, 1948, the United Nation's General Assembly adopted the *Declaration of Human Rights*.

Eleanor Roosevelt died on November 7, 1962.

Selected Reading

Black, Allida M., Editor, *Courage in a Dangerous World: The Political Writings of Eleanor Roosevelt*, 1999.

Douglas, Helen Gahagan, *The Eleanor Roosevelt We Remember*, 1963.

Hershan, Stella K., *The Candles She Lit: The Legacy of Eleanor Roosevelt*, 1993.

Lash, Joseph, *Eleanor: The Years Alone*, 1972.

Roosevelt, Eleanor, *On My Own*, 1958.

Franklin D. Roosevelt

Franklin Delano Roosevelt was born on January 30, 1882 in Hyde Park, New York, the child of James and Sara (Delano) Roosevelt. Educated at Harvard College and Columbia University Law School, Roosevelt, a Democrat, served as a New York State Senator (1910-13), Assistant U.S. Navy Secretary (1913-20), New York State Governor (1928-32), and President of the United States (1933-45). The two most significant events in the Roosevelt Presidency were The Great Depression (an economic crisis precipitated by the 1929 stock market crash) and the Second World War (precipitated by Japan's surprise attack on Pearl Harbor).

The Only Thing We Have To Fear Is Fear Itself
March 4, 1933

At the 1932 Democratic National Convention in Chicago, Illinois, candidate Franklin Roosevelt pledged *a "New Deal" for the American people*. In his First Inaugural Address, delivered on March 4, 1933, President Roosevelt began to make good on that *New Deal* pledge, outlining the specific steps he would take to lift America out of The Depression. At the same time, he reassured the American people in this landmark speech, *The only thing we have to fear is fear itself*.

The Day That Will Live In Infamy
December 8, 1941

On Sunday, December 7, 1941, the Japanese launched a devastating surprise attack against the U.S. Pacific Fleet at Pearl Harbor, Hawaii, in which 2,397 Americans were killed, 1,103 of them in the sinking of the battleship *Arizona*. The next day, President Franklin Roosevelt addressed a Joint Session of the United States Congress, requesting that they declare war against Japan, with this landmark speech - *Yesterday, December 7, 1941, a date which will live in infamy, the United States of America was suddenly and deliberately attacked by naval and air forces of the Empire of Japan.*

The Only Thing We Have To Fear Is Fear Itself

I am certain that my fellow Americans expect that on my induction into the Presidency I will address them with a candor and a decision which the present situation of our Nation impels. This is preeminently the time to speak the truth, the whole truth, frankly and boldly. Nor need we shrink from honestly facing conditions in our country today. This great Nation will endure as it has endured, will revive and will prosper. So, first of all, let me assert my firm belief that the only thing we have to fear is fear itself - nameless, unreasoning, unjustified terror which paralyzes needed efforts to convert retreat into advance. In every dark hour of our national life a leadership of frankness and vigor has met with that understanding and support of the people themselves which is essential to victory. I am convinced that you will again give that support to leadership in these critical days.

In such a spirit on my part and on yours we face our common difficulties. They concern, thank God, only material things. Values have shrunken to fantastic levels; taxes have risen; our ability to pay has fallen; government of all kinds is faced by serious curtailment of income; the means of exchange are frozen in the currents of trade; the withered leaves of industrial enterprise lie on every side; farmers find no markets for their produce; the savings of many years in thousands of families are gone.

More important, a host of unemployed citizens face the grim problem of existence, and an equally great number toil with little return. Only a foolish optimist can deny the dark realities of the moment.

Yet our distress comes from no failure of substance. We are stricken by no plague of locusts. Compared with the perils which our forefathers conquered because they believed and were not afraid, we have still much to be thankful for. Nature still offers her bounty and human efforts have multiplied it. Plenty is at our doorstep, but a generous use of it languishes in the very sight of the supply. Primarily this is because rulers of the exchange of mankind's goods have failed, through their own stubbornness and their own incompetence, have admitted their failure, and abdicated. Practices of the unscrupulous moneychangers stand indicted in the court of public opinion, rejected by the hearts and minds of men.

True they have tried, but their efforts have been cast in the pattern of an outworn tradition. Faced by failure of credit they have proposed only the lending of more money. Stripped of the lure of profit by which to induce our people to follow their false leadership, they have resorted to exhortations, pleading tearfully for restored confidence. They know only the rules of a generation of self-seekers. They have no vision, and when there is no vision the people perish.

The moneychangers have fled from their high seats in the temple of our civilization. We may now restore that temple to the ancient truths. The measure of the restoration lies in the extent to which we apply social values more noble than mere monetary profit.

Happiness lies not in the mere possession of money; it lies in the joy of achievement, in the thrill of creative effort. The joy and moral stimulation of work no longer must be forgotten in the mad chase of evanescent profits. These dark days will be worth all they cost us if they teach us that our true destiny is not to be ministered unto but to minister to ourselves and to our fellow men.

Recognition of the falsity of material wealth as the standard of success goes hand in hand with the abandonment of the false belief that public office and high political position are to be valued only by the standards of pride and place and personal profit; and there must be an end to a conduct in banking and in business which too often has given to a sacred trust the likeness of callous and selfish wrongdoing. Small wonder that confidence languishes, for it thrives only on honesty, on honor, on the sacredness of obligations, on faithful protection, on unselfish performance; without them it can not live.

Restoration calls, however, not for changes in ethics alone. This Nation asks for action, and action now.

Our greatest primary task is to put people to work. This is no unsolvable problem if we face it wisely and courageously. It can be accomplished in part by direct recruiting by the Government itself treating the task as we would treat the emergency of a war, but at the same time, through this employment, accomplishing greatly needed projects to stimulate and reorganize the use of our natural resources.

Hand in hand with this we must frankly recognize the overbalance of population in our industrial centers and, by engaging on a national scale in a redistribution, endeavor to provide a better use of the land for those best fitted for the land. The task can be helped by definite efforts to raise the values of agricultural products and with this the power to purchase the output of our cities. It can be helped by preventing realistically the tragedy of the growing loss through foreclosure of our small homes and our farms. It can be helped by insistence that the Federal, State, and local governments act forthwith on the demand that their cost be drastically reduced. It can be helped by the unifying of relief activities which today are often scattered, uneconomical, and unequal. It can be helped by national planning for and supervision of all forms of transportation and of communications and other utilities which have a definitely public character. There are many ways in which it can be helped, but it can never be helped merely by talking about it. We must act and act quickly.

Finally, in our progress toward a resumption of work we require two safeguards against a return of the evils of the old order; there must be a strict supervision of all banking and credits and investments; there must be an end to speculation with other people's money, and there must be provision for an adequate but sound currency.

There are the lines of attack. I shall presently urge upon a new Congress in special session detailed measure for their fulfillment, and I shall seek the immediate assistance of the several States.

Through this program of action we address ourselves to putting our own national house in order and making income balance outgo. Our international trade relations, though vastly important, are in point of time and necessity secondary to the establishment of a sound national economy. I favor as a practical policy the putting of first things first. I shall spare no effort to restore world trade by international economic readjustment, but the emergency at home cannot wait on that accomplishment.

The basic thought that guides these specific means of national recovery is not narrowly nationalistic. It is the insistence, as a first consideration, upon the interdependence of the various elements in all parts of the United States - a recognition of the old and permanently important manifestation of the American spirit of the pioneer. It is the way to recovery. It is the immediate way. It is the strongest assurance that the recovery will endure.

In the field of world policy I would dedicate this Nation to the policy of the good neighbor - the neighbor who resolutely respects himself and, because he does so, respects the rights of others - the neighbor who respects his obligations and respects the sanctity of his agreements in and with a world of neighbors.

If I read the temper of our people correctly, we now realize as we have never realized before our interdependence on each other - that we cannot merely take but we must give as well - that if we are to go forward, we must move as a trained and loyal army willing to sacrifice for the good of a common discipline, because without such discipline no progress is made, no leadership becomes effective. We are, I know, ready and willing to submit our lives and property to such discipline, because it makes possible a leadership which aims at a larger good. This I propose to offer, pledging that the larger purposes will bind upon us all as a sacred obligation with a unity of duty hitherto evoked only in time of armed strife.

With this pledge taken, I assume unhesitatingly the leadership of this great army of our people dedicated to a disciplined attack upon our common problems.

Action in this image and to this end is feasible under the form of government which we have inherited from our ancestors. Our Constitution is so simple and practical that it is possible always to meet extraordinary needs by changes in emphasis and arrangement without loss of essential form. That is why our constitutional system has proved itself the most superbly enduring political mechanism the modern world has produced. It has met every stress of vast expansion of territory, of foreign wars, of bitter internal strife, of world relations.

It is to be hoped that the normal balance of executive and legislative authority may be wholly adequate to meet the unprecedented task before us. But it may be that an unprecedented demand and need for undelayed action may call for temporary departure from that normal balance of public procedure.

I am prepared under my Constitutional duty to recommend the measures that a stricken nation in the midst of a stricken world may require. These measures, or such other measures as the Congress may build out of its experience and wisdom, I shall seek, within my constitutional authority, to bring to speedy adoption.

But in the event that the Congress shall fail to take one of these two courses, and in the event that the national emergency is still critical, I shall not evade the clear course of duty that will then confront me. I shall ask the Congress for the one remaining instrument to meet the crisis - broad Executive power to ware a war against the emergency, as great as the power that would be given to me if we were in fact invaded by a foreign foe.

For the trust reposed in me I will return the courage and the devotion that befit the time. I can do no less.

We face the arduous days that lie before us in the warm courage of the national unity; with the clear consciousness of seeking old and precious moral values; with the clean satisfaction that comes from the stern performance of duty by old and young alike. We aim at the assurance of a rounded and permanent national life.

We do not distrust the future of essential democracy. The people of the United States have not failed. In their need they have registered a mandate that they want direct, vigorous action. They have asked for discipline and direction under leadership. They have made me the present instrument of their wishes. In the spirit of the gift I take it.

In this dedication of a Nation we humbly ask the blessing of God. May He protect each and every one of us. May He guide me in the days to come.

The Day That Will Live In Infamy

Yesterday, December 7, 1941, a date which will live in infamy, the United States of America was suddenly and deliberately attacked by naval and air forces of the Empire of Japan.

The United States was at peace with that nation and, at the solicitation of Japan, was still in conversation with its Government and its Emperor, looking toward the maintenance of peace in the Pacific.

Indeed, one hour after Japanese air squadrons had commenced bombing Oahu, the Japanese Ambassador to the United States and his colleague delivered to the Secretary of State a formal reply to a recent American message. While this reply stated that it seemed useless to continue the existing diplomatic negotiations, it contained no threat or hint of war or armed attack.

It will be recorded that the distance of Hawaii from Japan makes it obvious that the attack was deliberately planned many days or even weeks ago. During the intervening time, the Japanese Government has deliberately sought to deceive the United States by false statements and expressions of hope for continued peace.

The attack yesterday on the Hawaiian Islands has caused severe damage to American naval and military forces. Very many American lives have been lost. In addition, American ships have been reported torpedoed on the high seas between San Francisco and Honolulu.

Yesterday the Japanese Government also launched an attack against Malaya. Last night Japanese forces attacked Hong Kong. Last night Japanese forces attacked Guam. Last night Japanese forces attacked the Philippine Islands. Last night the Japanese attacked Wake Island. This morning the Japanese attacked Midway Island.

Japan has, therefore, undertaken a surprise offensive extending throughout the Pacific area. The facts of yesterday speak for themselves. The people of the United States have already formed their opinions and well understand the implications to the very life and safety of our nation.

As Commander-in-Chief of the Army and Navy, I have directed that all measures be taken for our defense.

Always will we remember the character of the onslaught against us. No matter how long it may take us to overcome this premeditated invasion, the American people in their righteous might will win through to absolute victory.

I believe I interpret the will of the Congress and of the people when I assert that we will not only defend ourselves to the uttermost but will make very certain that this form of treachery shall never endanger us again.

Hostilities exist. There is no blinking at the fact that our people, our territory, and our interests are in grave danger. With confidence in our armed forces - with the unbounding determination of our people - we will gain the inevitable triumph, so help us God.

I ask that the Congress declare that since the unprovoked and dastardly attack by Japan on Sunday, December 7, a state of war has existed between the United States and the Japanese Empire.

Franklin D. Roosevelt

Afterward

President Roosevelt's New Deal produced government programs - the National Recovery Act, the Social Security Act, the Federal Securities Act, the National Labor Relations Act, and the Minimum Wage Act - all designed to end the Great Depression.

On December 8, 1941, the United States Congress declared war on Japan. Three days later Japan's ally, Nazi Germany, declared war on the United States. President Roosevelt's leadership was crucial to the waging of the war and the winning of the peace.

Franklin Roosevelt died on April 12, 1945.

Selected Reading

Abbott, Philip, *The Exemplary Presidency: Franklin D. Roosevelt and the American Political Tradition*, 1990.

Davis, Kenneth S., *FDR, Into the Storm, 1937-1940: A History*, 1993.

Einaudi, Mario, *The Roosevelt Revolution*, 1959.

Gies, Joseph, *Franklin D. Roosevelt: Portrait of a President*, 1971.

Goodwin, Doris Kearns, *No Ordinary Time: Franklin and Eleanor Roosevelt: The Home Front in World War II*, 1994.

Leuchtenburg, William E., Editor, *Franklin D. Roosevelt: A Profile*, 1968.

Roosevelt, Elliott, *As He Saw It*, 1946.

Rusbridger, James, and Eric Nave, *Betrayal at Pearl Harbor: How Churchill Lured Roosevelt into World War II*, 1991.

Schlesinger, Arthur M., *The Age of Roosevelt*, 1960.

Waller, George M., Editor, *Pearl Harbor: Roosevelt and the Coming of the War*, 1965.

Nicola Sacco & Bartolomeo Vanzetti
Sentenced To Death
April 19, 1927

The Department of Justice has undertaken to rid America of radicals, socialists, anarchists, and other moral perverts.
- U.S. Attorney General Palmer, 1920

On January 2, 1920, the first *Palmer Raids*, mass arrests of *radicals, socialists, anarchists, and other moral perverts*, were conducted nationwide. Singled out for special attention were a group of Italian-born radical anarchists living in Massachusetts who had, as part of their avowed revolutionary tactics, attempted to kill the U.S. Attorney General. In 1921 two of these radical anarchists, Nicola Sacco and Bartolomeo Vanzetti, were arrested and tried, not for their radical activities, but on trumped-up murder charges.

Nicola Sacco was born on April 22, 1891 in Torremagiore, Italy, the child of Michele and Angela (Mosmacotelli) Sacco. He immigrated to America in 1908 and settled in Milford, Massachusetts. Bartolomeo Vanzetti was born on June 11, 1888 in Villafalletto, Italy, the child of Giovan and Giovanna (Nivello) Vanzetti. He immigrated to America in 1908 and settled in Plymouth, Massachusetts.

In 1920 a double murder was committed in Braintree, Massachusetts. Sacco and Vanzetti were arrested for the crime. Their trial, held at the Dedham Courthouse from May 31 to July 14, 1921, was characterized by perjured testimony and false evidence. They pled innocent and were found guilty.

On April 19, 1927, after all legal appeals to save their lives were exhausted, Nicola Sacco and Bartolomeo Vanzetti were returned to the Dedham Courthouse. In answer to the Judge's question - *Have you anything to say why a death sentence should not be passed upon you?* - Sacco and then Vanzetti delivered these landmark speeches proclaiming their innocence.

Nicola Sacco & Bartolomeo Vanzetti

Nicola Sacco: I am not an orator. It is not very familiar with me the English language, and, as I know, as my friend has told me, my comrade Vanzetti will speak more long, so I thought to give him the chance.

I never know, never heard, even read in history anything so cruel as this court. After seven years prosecuting, they still consider us guilty. And these gentle people here are arrayed with us in this court today. I know the sentence will be between two class, the oppressed class and the rich class, and there will be always collision between one and the other. We fraternize the people with the books, with the literature. You persecute the people, tyrannize over them, and kill them. We try the education of people always. You try to put a path between us and some other nationality that hates each other. That is why I am here today on this bench, for having been the oppressed class. Well, you are the oppressor.

You know it, Judge Thayer - you know all my life, you know why I have been here, and after seven years that you have been persecuting me and my poor wife, and you still today abuse us to death. I would like to tell you my life, but what is the use? You know all about what I say before, and my friend - that is, my comrade - will be talking, because he is more familiar with the language, and I will give him a chance. My comrade, the man kind, the kind man to all the children, you sentence him two times, in the Bridgewater case and the Dedham case, connected with me, and you know he is innocent. You forget all the population that has been with us for seven years, to sympathize and give us all their energy and all their kindness. You do not care for them. Among that peoples and the comrades and the working class, there is a big legion of intellectual people which have been with us for seven years, but to not commit the iniquitous sentence, but still the court goes ahead. And I think I thank you all, you peoples, my comrades who have been with me for seven years, with the Sacco-Vanzetti case, and I will give my friend a chance.

I forget one thing which my comrade remember me. As I said before, Judge Thayer know all my life, and he know that I am never be guilty, never - not yesterday nor today nor forever.

Bartolomeo Vanzetti: What I say is that I am innocent, not only of the Braintree crime, but also of the Bridgewater crime. That I am not only innocent of these two crimes, but in all my life I have never stole and I have never killed and I have never spilled blood. That is what I want to say. And it is not all. Not only am I innocent of these two crimes, not only in all my life I have never stole, never killed, never spilled blood, but I have struggled all my life, since I began to reason, to eliminate crime from the earth.

Everybody that knows these two arms knows very well that I did not need to go in between the streets and kill a man to make the money. I can live with my two arms, and live well. But besides that, I can live even without work with my arm for other people. I have had plenty of chance to live independently and to live what the world conceives to be a higher life than not to gain our bread with the sweat of our brow.

. . . . What I want to say is this - everybody ought to understand that the first of the defense has been terrible. My first lawyer did not stick to defend us. He had made no work to collect witnesses and evidence in our favor. The record in the Plymouth court is a pity. I am told that they are almost gone - half lost. So the defense had a tremendous work to do in order to collect some evidence, to collect some testimony to offset and to learn what the testimony of the state has done. And in this consideration it take double time of the state without delay, double time that they delay the case it would have been reasonable, whereas it took less than the state. Well, I have already say that I am not guilty of these two crimes, but I never commit a crime in my life - I have never steal and I have never kill and I have never spilled blood, and I have fought against the crime, and I have fought and I have sacrificed myself even to eliminate the crimes that the law and the church legitimate and sanctify.

That is what I say - I would not wish to a dog or a snake, to the most low and misfortunate creature of the earth - I would not wish to any of them what I have had to suffer for things that I am not guilty of. But my conviction is that I have suffered for things that I am guilty of. I am suffering because I am a radical, and indeed I am a radical; I have suffered because I was an Italian, and indeed I am an Italian; I have suffered more for my family and for my beloved than for myself; but I am so convinced to be right that if you would execute me two times, and if I could be reborn two other times, I would live again to do what I have done already.

Afterward

Nicola Sacco and Bartolomeo Vanzetti were executed on August 23, 1927.

Selected Reading

Ehrmann, Herbert B., *The Untried Case: The Sacco-Vanzetti Case and the Morelli Gang*, 1933.

Fraenkel, Osmond K., *The Sacco-Vanzetti Case*, 1990.

Frankfurter, Felix, *The Case of Sacco and Vanzetti: A Critical Analysis for Lawyers and Laymen*, 1962.

Lyons, Eugene, *The Life and Death of Sacco and Vanzetti*, 1970.

Young, William, and David E. Kaiser, *Postmortem: New Evidence in the Case of Sacco and Vanzetti*, 1985.

Margaret Sanger
The Morality Of Birth Control
November 18, 1921

Mothers! Can you afford to have a large family? Do you want any more children? If not, why do you have them? Safe, harmless birth control information can be obtained free from trained nurses.
- Margaret Sanger, *Birth Control Flyer,* 1916

Margaret Higgins Sanger was born on September 14, 1879 in Corning, New York, the child of Michael and Anne (Purcell) Higgins. Educated as a obstetrical nurse, Sanger was an eyewitness to the medical, emotional, and financial toll unplanned pregnancies had on poor women - *I saw women writhing in travail to bring forth little babies, the babies themselves naked and hungry, wrapped in newspapers to keep them from the cold.* Margaret Sanger began to speak on *birth control* - a term she herself coined. On November 13, 1921, in New York City's Town Hall, Sanger tried to deliver a speech entitled *The Morality Of Birth Control.* She was arrested on a charge of disorderly conduct. The next day, the New York *Times* headline read, *Birth Control Raid Made On Archbishop's Order.* The newspaper reported that Sanger's arrest had been ordered by New York's Roman Catholic Archbishop, Patrick Hayes, on moral grounds - *To take life after its inception is a horrible crime; but to prevent human life that the Creator is about to bring into being is satanic.* The charge was dismissed and Sanger was released, but the ensuing controversy over the Catholic Church's attempt to deny Margaret Sanger her First Amendment rights served to popularize and legitimize her birth control message. The New York *World* wrote, *The issue is bigger than the right of Margaret Sanger to advocate birth control. It is part of the eternal fight for free speech and free assembly which must always find defenders if freedom is to survive.*

On November 18, 1921, at New York City's Park Theater, Margaret Sanger delivered this landmark speech on family planning, *The Morality Of Birth Control.*

Religious propaganda against birth control is crammed with contradiction and fallacy. It refutes itself. Yet it brings the opposing views into vivid contrast. In stating these differences we should make clear that advocates of birth control are not seeking to attack the Catholic Church. We quarrel with that Church, however, when it seeks to assume authority over non-Catholics and to dub their behavior immoral because they do not conform to the dictatorship of Rome. The question of bearing and rearing children we hold is the concern of the mother and the potential mother. If she delegates the responsibility, the ethical education, to an external authority, that is her affair. We object, however, to the State or the Church which appoints itself as arbiter and dictator in this sphere and attempts to force unwilling women into compulsory maternity.

When Catholics declare that *the authorities at Rome have again and again declared that all positive methods of this nature are immoral and forbidden,* they do so upon the assumption that morality consists in conforming to laws laid down and enforced by external authority, in submission to decrees and dicta imposed from without. In this case, they decide in a wholesale manner the conduct of millions, demanding of them not the intelligent exercise of their own individual judgment and discrimination, but unquestioning submission and conformity to dogma. The Church thus takes the place of all-powerful parents, and demands of its children merely that they should obey. In my belief, such a philosophy hampers the development of individual intelligence. Morality then becomes a more or less successful attempt to conform to a code, instead of an attempt to bring reason and intelligence to bear upon the solution of each individual human problem.

But, we read on, birth control methods are not merely contrary to *moral law*, but forbidden because they are *unnatural*, being *the perversion of a natural function*. This, of course, is the weakest link in the whole chain. Yet *there is no question of the lawfulness of birth restriction through abstinence* - as though abstinence itself were not unnatural! For more than a thousand years, the Church was occupied with the problem of imposing abstinence on its priesthood, its most educated and trained body of men, educated to look upon asceticism as the finest ideal; it took one thousand years to convince the Catholic priesthood that abstinence was *natural* or practicable. Nevertheless, there is still this talk of abstinence, self-control, and self-denial, almost in the same breath with the condemnation of birth control as *unnatural*.

If it is our duty to act as *cooperators with the Creator* to bring children into the world, it is difficult to say at what point our behavior is *unnatural*. If it is immoral and *unnatural* to prevent an unwanted life from coming into existence, is it not immoral and *unnatural* to remain unmarried from the age of puberty? Such casuistry is unconvincing and feeble. We need only point out that rational intelligence is also a *natural* function, and that it is as imperative for us to use the faculties of judgment, criticism, discrimination of choice, selection, and control, all the faculties of the intelligence, as it is to use those of reproduction. It is certainly dangerous *to frustrate the natural ends for which these faculties were created.* This, also, is always intrinsically wrong - as wrong as lying and blasphemy - and infinitely more devastating. Intelligence is as natural to us as any other faculty, and it is fatal to moral development and growth to refuse to use it and to delegate to others the solution of our individual problems. The evil will not be that one's conduct is divergent from current and conventional moral codes. There may be every outward evidence of conformity, but this agreement may be arrived at by the restriction and suppression of subjective desires and the more or less successful attempt at mere conformity. Such *morality* would conceal an inner conflict. The fruits of this conflict would be neurosis and hysteria on the one hand, or concealed gratification of suppressed desires on the other, with a resultant hypocrisy and cant. True morality cannot be based on conformity. There must be no conflict between subjective desire and outward behavior.

To object to these traditional and churchly ideas does not by any means imply that the doctrine of birth control is anti-Christian. On the contrary, it may be profoundly in accordance with the Sermon on the Mount. One of the greatest living theologians and most penetrating students of the problems of civilization is of this opinion. In an address delivered before the Eugenics Education Society of London, William Ralph Inge, the Very Reverend Dean of St. Paul's Cathedral, London, pointed out that the doctrine of birth control was to be interpreted as of the very essence of Christianity.

. . . . Dean Inge believes birth control is an essential part of eugenics, and an essential part of Christian morality. On this point he asserts,

We do wish to remind our orthodox and conservative friends that the Sermon on the Mount contains some admirably clear and unmistakable eugenic precepts - 'Do men gather grapes of thorns, or figs of thistles? A corrupt tree cannot bring forth good fruit; neither can a good tree bring forth evil fruit. Every tree which bringeth not forth good fruit is hewn down and cast into the fire.' We wish to apply these words not only to the actions of individuals, which spring from their characters, but to the character of individuals, which spring from their inherited qualities. This extension of the scope of the maxim seems to me quite legitimate. Men do not gather grapes of thorns. As our proverb says, you cannot make a silk purse out of a sow's ear. If we believe this - and do not act upon it by trying to move public opinion towards giving social reform, education, and religion a better material to work upon - we are sinning against the light, and not doing our best to bring in the Kingdom of God upon earth.

As long as sexual activity is regarded in a dualistic and contradictory light - in which it is revealed either as the instrument by which men and women *cooperate with the Creator* to bring children into the world, on the one hand, and on the other as the sinful instrument of self-gratification, lust, and sensuality - there is bound to be an endless conflict in human conduct, producing ever increasing misery, pain, and injustice. In crystallizing and codifying this contradiction, the Church not only solidified its own power over men but reduced women to the most abject and prostrate slavery. It was essentially a morality that would not *work*. The sex instinct in the human race is too strong to be bound by the dictates of any church. The Church's failure, its century after century of failure, is now evident on every side, for, having convinced men and women that only in its baldly propagative phase is sexual expression legitimate, the teachings of the Church have driven sex underground, into secret channels, strengthened the conspiracy of silence, concentrated men's thoughts upon the *lusts of the body* - have sown, cultivated, and reaped a crop of bodily and mental diseases, and developed a society congenitally and almost hopelessly unbalanced. How is any progress to be made - how is any human expression or education possible when women and men are taught to combat and resist their natural impulses and to despise their bodily functions?

Humanity, we are glad to realize, is rapidly freeing itself from this *morality* imposed upon it by its self-appointed and self-perpetuating masters. From a hundred different points the imposing edifice of this *morality* has been and is being attacked. Sincere and thoughtful defenders and exponents of the teachings of Christ now acknowledge the falsity of the traditional codes and their malignant influence upon the moral and physical well-being of humanity.

Ecclesiastical opposition to birth control on the part of certain representatives of the Protestant churches, based usually on quotations from the Bible, is equally invalid, and for the same reason. The attitude of the more intelligent and enlightened clergy has been well and succinctly expressed by Dean Inge, who, referring to the ethics of birth control, writes, *This is emphatically a matter in which every man and woman must judge for themselves, and must refrain from judging others.* We must not neglect the important fact that it is not merely in the practical results of such a decision - not in the small number of children - not even in the healthier and better cared for children - not in the possibility of elevating the living conditions of the individual family - that the ethical value of birth control alone lies. Precisely because the practice of birth control does demand the exercise of decision, the making of choice, the use of the reasoning powers, is it an instrument of moral education as well as of hygienic and racial advance. It awakens the attention of parents to their potential children. It forces upon the individual consciousness the question of the standards of living. In a profound manner, it protects and reasserts the inalienable rights of the child-to-be.

Psychology and the outlook of modern life are stressing the growth of independent responsibility and discrimination as the true basis of ethics. The old traditional morality, with its train of vice, disease, promiscuity and prostitution, is in reality dying out, killing itself off because it is too irresponsible and too dangerous to individual and social well-being. The transition from the old to the new, like all fundamental changes, is fraught with many dangers. But it is a revolution that cannot be stopped.

The smaller family, with its lower infant mortality rate, is, in more definite and concrete manner than many actions outwardly deemed *moral*, the expression of moral judgment and responsibility. It is the assertion of a standard of living, inspired by the wish to obtain a fuller and more expressive life for the children than the parents have enjoyed. If the morality or immorality of any course of conduct is to be determined by the motives which inspire it, there is evidently at the present day no higher morality than the intelligent practice of birth control.

The immorality of many who practice birth control lies in not daring to preach what they practice. What is the secret of the hypocrisy of the well-to-do, who are willing to contribute generously to charities and philanthropies, who spend thousands annually in the upkeep and sustenance of the delinquent, the defective, and the dependent, and yet join the conspiracy of silence that prevents the poorer classes from learning how to improve their conditions and elevate their standards of living? It is as though they were to cry, *We'll give you anything except the thing you ask for - the means whereby you may become responsible and self-reliant in your own lives.*

The brunt of this injustice falls on women, because the old traditional morality is the invention of men. *No religion, no physical or moral code,* wrote the clear-sighted George Drysdale, *proposed by one sex for the other, can be really suitable. Each must work out its laws for itself in every department of life.* In the moral code developed by the Church, women have been so degraded that they have been habituated to look upon themselves through the eyes of men. Very imperfectly have women developed their own self-consciousness, the realization of their tremendous and supreme position in civilization. Women can develop this power only in one way - by the exercise of responsibility - by the exercise of judgment, reason, or discrimination. They need ask for no *rights*. They need only assert power. Only by the exercise of self-guidance and intelligent self-direction can that inalienable, supreme, pivotal power be expressed. More than ever in history, women need to realize that nothing can ever come to us from another. Everything we attain we must owe to ourselves. Our own spirit must vitalize it. Our own heart must feel it. For we are not passive machines. We are not to be lectured, guided, and molded this way or that. We are alive and intelligent, we women, no less than men, and we must awaken to the essential realization that we are living beings, endowed with will, choice, comprehension, and that every step in life must be taken at our own initiative.

Moral and sexual balance in civilization will only be established by the assertion and expression of power on the part of women. This power will not be found in any futile seeking for economic independence or in the aping of men in industrial and business pursuits, nor by joining battle for the so-called *single standard*. Woman's power can only be expressed and make itself felt when she refuses the task of bringing unwanted children into the world to be exploited in industry and slaughtered in wars. When we refuse to produce battalions of babies to be exploited - when we declare to the nation,

Show us that the best possible chance in life is given to every child now brought into the world, before you cry for more! At present our children are a glut on the market. You hold infant life cheap.

Help us to make the world a fit place for children. When you have done this, we will bear you children - then we shall be true women.

The new morality will express this power and responsibility on the part of women.

With the realization of the moral responsibility of women, writes Havelock Ellis, *the natural relations of life spring back to their due biological adjustment. Motherhood is restored to its natural sacredness. It becomes the concern of the woman herself, and not of society nor any individual, to determine the conditions under which the child shall be conceived. . . .*

Moreover, woman shall further assert her power by refusing to remain the passive instrument of sensual self-gratification on the part of men. Birth control, in philosophy and practice, is the destroyer of that dualism of the old sexual code. It denies that the sole purpose of sexual activity is procreation; it also denies that sex should be reduced to the level of sensual lust, or that woman should permit herself to be the instrument of its satisfaction. In increasing and differentiating her love demands, woman must elevate sex into another sphere, whereby it may subserve and enhance the possibility of individual and human expression. Man will gain in this no less than woman, for in the age-old enslavement of woman he has enslaved himself, and in the liberation of womankind, all of humanity will experience the joys of a new and fuller freedom.

. . . . The moral justification and ethical necessity of birth control need not be empirically based upon the mere approval of experience and custom. Its morality is more profound. Birth control is an ethical necessity for humanity today because it places in our hands a new instrument of self-expression and self-realization. It gives us control over one of the primordial forces of nature, to which in the past the majority of mankind have been enslaved, and by which it has been cheapened and debased. It arouses us to the possibility of newer and greater freedom. It develops the power, the responsibility and intelligence to use this freedom in living a liberated and abundant life. It permits us to enjoy this liberty without danger of infringing upon the similar liberty of our fellow men, or of injuring and curtailing the freedom of the next generation. It shows us that we need not seek in the amassing of worldly wealth, nor in the illusion of some extraterrestrial Heaven or earthly Utopia of a remote future the road to human development. The Kingdom of Heaven is in a very definite sense within us. Not by leaving our body and our fundamental humanity behind us, not by aiming to be anything but what we are, shall we become ennobled or immortal. By knowing ourselves, by expressing ourselves, by realizing ourselves more completely than has ever before been possible, not only shall we attain the Kingdom ourselves, but we shall hand on the torch of life undimmed to our children and the children of our children.

Afterward

Margaret Sanger used her new fame to found America's first successful birth control clinic, New York City's Birth Control Research Bureau. In 1942 Sanger's American Birth Control League was renamed Planned Parenthood Federation of America. In 1952 Sanger began to raise funds for the research into *anti-fertility* drugs, which resulted in the invention of the first oral contraceptive. In 1963 Sanger said in an interview, *Fifty years ago I realized what was coming - the population explosion we hear so much about today, women having more and more babies until there's neither food nor room for them on earth. I tried to do something about it. Now, thousands of people all over the world are aware of the problem and its only possible solutions - family limitation and planned parenthood.*

Margaret Sanger died on September 6, 1966.

Selected Reading

Chesler, Ellen, *Woman of Valor: Margaret Sanger and the Birth Control Movement in America*, 1992.

Douglas, Emily Taft, *Margaret Sanger, Pioneer of the Future*, 1975.

Gray, Madeline, *Margaret Sanger: A Biography of the Champion of Birth Control*, 1979.

Hersey, Harold, *Margaret Sanger: The Biography of Birth Control*, 1938.

Kennedy, David, *Birth Control in America: The Career of Margaret Sanger*, 1970.

Lader, Lawrence, *The Margaret Sanger Story and the Fight for Birth Control*, 1973.

Sanger, Margaret, *Margaret Sanger: An Autobiography*, 1999.

———, *My Fight for Birth Control*, 1931.

Benjamin Spock
A Call To Resist Illegitimate Authority
October 12, 1967

The United States Government cannot tolerate the kind of rebellion Dr. Spock represents - a revolt in the ranks of the older generation, especially those with some status and influence. It cannot fill its prisons with doctors and clergymen without losing credibility.,
- The Nation Magazine, 1967

On October 12, 1967, Benjamin Spock, *America's Baby Doctor*, issued a landmark anti-war/anti-draft statement, *A Call To Resist Illegitimate Authority*, as part of his personal crusade against America's deepening involvement in the Vietnam War. For this statement, as well as acts of nonviolent civil disobedience, which led to his arrests in New York City and Washington, D.C., the Federal Government charged Benjamin Spock with criminal conspiracy for having *counseled, aided, and abetted resistance to the draft.*

Benjamin McLane Spock was born on May 2, 1903 in New Haven, Connecticut, the child of Benjamin, Sr. and Mildred (Stoughton) Spock. Educated at Yale University and Columbia University's Medical School, Dr. Spock, a pediatrician, published in 1946 the national bestseller *The Common Sense Book of Baby and Child Care* (later renamed *Dr. Spock's Baby and Child Care*). In the 1960's, he came out of retirement to become an outspoken critic of the Vietnam War - *What is the use of doctors trying to help parents bring up healthy children to have them killed in such an ignoble cause?*

Benjamin Spock was found guilty of criminal conspiracy for having issued *A Call To Resist Illegitimate Authority*. The trial Judge wrote, *Dr. Spock should not escape under the guise of free speech.* The conviction was later overturned by the U.S. Court of Appeals, which wrote, *Dr. Spock's vigorous criticism of the draft and of the Vietnam War is free speech protected by the First Amendment, even though its effect is to interfere with the war effort.*

Benjamin Spock

To the young men of America, to the whole of the American people, and to all men of good will everywhere:

An ever growing number of young American men are finding that the American war in Vietnam so outrages their deepest moral and religious sense that they cannot contribute to it in any way. We share their moral outrage.

We further believe that the war is unconstitutional and illegal. Congress has not declared a war as required by the Constitution. Moreover, under the Constitution, treaties signed by the President and ratified by the Senate have the same force as the Constitution itself. The Charter of the United Nations is such a treaty. The Charter specifically obligates the United States to refrain from force or the threat of force in international relations. It requires member states to exhaust every peaceful means of settling disputes and to submit disputes which cannot be settled peacefully to the Security Council. The United States has systematically violated all of these Charter provisions for thirteen years.

Moreover, this war violates international agreements, treaties, and principles of law which the United States Government has solemnly endorsed. The combat role of the United States troops in Vietnam violates the Geneva Accords of 1954 which our government pledged to support but has since subverted. The destruction of rice, crops and livestock; the burning and bulldozing of entire villages consisting exclusively of civilian structures; the interning of civilian non-combatants in concentration camps; the summary executions of civilians in captured villages who could not produce satisfactory evidence of their loyalties or did not wish to be removed to concentration camps; the slaughter of peasants who dared to stand up in their fields and shake their fists at American helicopters - these are all actions of the kind which the United States and the other victorious powers of World War II declared to be crimes against humanity for which individuals were to be held personally responsible even when acting under the orders of their governments and for which Germans were sentenced at Nuremberg to long prison terms and death. The prohibition of such acts as war crimes was incorporated in treaty law by the Geneva Conventions of 1949, ratified by the United States. These are commitments to other countries and to mankind, and they would claim our allegiance even if Congress should declare war.

We also believe it is an unconstitutional denial of religious liberty and equal protection of the laws to withhold draft exemption from men whose religious or profound philosophical beliefs are opposed to what in the Western religious tradition have been long known as unjust wars.

Therefore, we believe on all these grounds that every free man has a legal right and a moral duty to exert every effort to end this war, to avoid collusion with it, and to encourage others to do the same. Young men in the armed forces or threatened with the draft face the most excruciating choices. For them various forms of resistance risk separation from their families and their country, destruction of their careers, loss of their freedom and loss of their lives. Each must choose the course of resistance dictated by his conscience and circumstances. Among those already in the armed forces some are refusing to obey specific illegal and immoral orders, some are attempting to educate their fellow servicemen on the murderous and barbarous nature of the war, some are absenting themselves without official leave. Among those not in the armed forces some are applying for status as conscientious objectors to American aggression in Vietnam, some are refusing to be inducted. Among both groups some are resisting openly and paying a heavy penalty, some are organizing more resistance within the United States, and some have sought sanctuary in other countries.

We believe that each of these forms of resistance against illegitimate authority is courageous and justified. Many of us believe that open resistance to the war and the draft is the course of action most likely to strengthen the moral resolve with which all of us can oppose the war and most likely to bring an end to the war.

We will continue to lend our support to those who undertake resistance to this war. We will raise funds to organize draft resistance unions, to supply legal defense and bail, to support families, and otherwise aid resistance to the war in whatever ways may seem appropriate.

We firmly believe that our statement is the sort of speech that under the First Amendment must be free, and that the actions we will undertake are as legal as is the war resistance of the young men themselves. In any case, we feel that we cannot shrink from fulfilling our responsibilities to the youth whom many of us teach, to the country whose freedom we cherish, and to the ancient traditions of religion and philosophy which we strive to preserve in this generation.

We call upon all men of good will to join us in this confrontation with immoral authority. Especially we call upon the universities to fulfill their mission of enlightenment and religious organizations to honor their heritage of brotherhood. Now is the time to resist.

Afterward

Dr. Spock remained politically active the rest of his life, working for international peace, civil rights, and social justice. He continued, when necessary, to resist authority.

Benjamin Spock died on March 15, 1998.

Selected Reading

Bloom, Lynn Z., *Doctor Spock*, 1972.
Maier, Thomas, *Dr. Spock: An American Life*, 1998.
Michalek, Irene R., *When Mercy Seasons Justice: The Spock Trial*, 1972.
Spock, Benjamin, and Mary Morgan, *Spock on Spock*, 1989.

Harry Truman
Hiroshima
August 6, 1945

*We call upon the Government of Japan to unconditionally surrender.
The alternative for Japan is prompt and utter destruction.*
- The Potsdam Declaration, July 26, 1945

At 8:15 a.m. EST on August 6, 1945, a U.S. Army Air Force
B-29 bomber, *The Enola Gay*, dropped an atomic bomb
(code name *Little Boy*) on the Japanese city of Hiroshima,
killing 80,000 and injuring an additional 80,000. The decision to use the atomic bomb to force Japan to unconditionally surrender was made by President Harry S. Truman.

Harry S. Truman was born on May 8, 1884 in Lamar, Missouri, the child of John and Martha (Young) Truman. After
several business failures, Truman entered politics, serving as
a County Judge, Missouri's U.S. Senator, and Vice President
of the United States. After the death of President Roosevelt elevated Harry Truman to the Presidency, he learned of
the existence of the Manhattan Project, the 5-year, 2-½
billion dollar effort which had built, and, on July 16, 1945,
successfully tested, the world's first atomic bomb. Ten days
later, the Allied *Potsdam Declaration* demanded that Japan unconditionally surrender or face *utter destruction*. If Japan refused, President Truman was faced with two war-ending
options - *Operation Downfall*, an invasion of Japan which
planners estimated would cost 1 million American casualties, including 250,000 killed - or the use of the Manhattan
Project's two remaining atomic bombs, code named *Little
Boy* and *Fat Man*. On July 30, 1945, Japan officially refused
to surrender. On July 31 President Truman weighed his options and decided, *A quarter of a million American soldiers are
worth a couple of Japanese cities.*

On August 6, 1945, President Harry Truman addressed the
nation in this landmark speech, announcing the atomic destruction of *Hiroshima*.

Sixteen hours ago, an American airplane dropped one bomb on Hiroshima, an important Japanese Army base. That bomb had more power than 20,000 tons of T.N.T. It had more than two thousand times the blast power of the British *Grand Slam,* which is the largest bomb ever yet used in the history of warfare.

The Japanese began the war from the air at Pearl Harbor. They have been repaid manifold. And the end is not yet. With this bomb, we have now added a new and revolutionary increase in destruction to supplement the growing power of our armed forces. In their present form, these bombs are now in production and even more powerful forms are in development.

It is an atomic bomb. It is a harnessing of the basic power of the universe. The force from which the sun draws its power has been loosed against those who brought war to the Far East.

Before 1939, it was the accepted belief of scientists that it was theoretically possible to release atomic energy. But no one knew any practical method of doing it. By 1942, however, we knew that the Germans were working feverishly to find a way to add atomic energy to the other engines of war with which they hoped to enslave the world. But they failed. We may be grateful to Providence that the Germans got the V-1's and V-2's late and in limited quantities and even more grateful that they did not get the atomic bomb at all. The battle of the laboratories held fateful risks for us as well as the battles of the air, land, and sea, and we have now won the battle of the laboratories as we have won the other battles. Beginning in 1940, before Pearl Harbor, scientific knowledge useful in war was pooled between the United States and Great Britain, and many priceless helps to our victories have come from that arrangement. Under that general policy the research on the atomic bomb was begun. With American and British scientists working together, we entered the race of discovery against the Germans.

The United States had available the large number of scientists of distinction in the many needed areas of knowledge. It had the tremendous industrial and financial resources necessary for the project, and they could be devoted to it without undue impairment of other vital war work. In the United States the laboratory work and the production plants, on which a substantial start had already been made, would be out of reach of enemy bombing, while at that time Britain was exposed to constant air attack and was still threatened with the possibility of invasion. For these reasons Prime Minister Churchill and President Roosevelt agreed that it was wise to carry on the project here. We now have two great plants and many lesser works devoted to the production of atomic power. Employment during peak construction numbered 125,000, and over 65,000 individuals are even now engaged in operating the plants. Many have worked there for two and a half years. Few know what they have been producing. They see great quantities of material going in and they see nothing coming out of these plants, for the physical size of the explosive charge is exceedingly small. We have spent two billion dollars on the greatest scientific gamble in history - and won.

But the greatest marvel is not the size of the enterprise, its secrecy, nor its cost, but the achievement of scientific brains in putting together infinitely complex pieces of knowledge held by many men in different fields of science into a workable plan. And hardly less marvelous has been the capacity of industry to design, and of labor to operate, the machines and methods to do things never done before so that the brainchild of many minds came forth in physical shape and performed as it was supposed to do. Both science and industry worked under the direction of the United States Army, which achieved a unique success in managing so diverse a problem in the advancement of knowledge in an amazingly short time. It is doubtful if such another combination could be got together in the world. What has been done is the greatest achievement of organized science in history. It was done under high pressure and without failure.

We are now prepared to obliterate more rapidly and completely every productive enterprise the Japanese have above ground in any city. We shall destroy their docks, their factories, and their communications. Let there be no mistake - we shall completely destroy Japan's power to make war.

It was to spare the Japanese people from utter destruction that the ultimatum of July 26 was issued at Potsdam. Their leaders promptly rejected that ultimatum. If they do not now accept our terms, they may expect a rain of ruin from the air, the like of which has never been seen on this earth. Behind this air attack will follow sea and land forces in such numbers and power as they have not yet seen and with the fighting skill of which they are already well aware. The Secretary of War, who has kept in personal touch with all phases of the project, will immediately make public a statement giving further details. His statement will give facts concerning the sites at Oak Ridge near Knoxville, Tennessee, and at Richland near Pasco, Washington, and an installation near Santa Fe, New Mexico. Although the workers at the sites have been making materials to be used in producing the greatest destructive force in history, they have not themselves been in danger beyond that of many other occupations, for the utmost care has been taken of their safety.

The fact that we can release atomic energy ushers in a new era in man's understanding of nature's forces. Atomic energy may in the future supplement the power that now comes from coal, oil, and falling water, but at present it cannot be produced on a basis to compete with them commercially. Before that comes, there must be a long period of intensive research.

It has never been the habit of the scientists of this country or the policy of this Government to withhold from the world scientific knowledge. Normally, therefore, everything about the work with atomic energy would be made public. But under present circumstances it is not intended to divulge the technical processes of production or all the military applications, pending further examination of possible methods of protecting us and the rest of the world from the danger of sudden destruction.

I shall recommend that the Congress of the United States consider promptly the establishment of an appropriate commission to control the production and use of atomic power within the United States. I shall give further consideration and make further recommendations to the Congress as to how atomic power can become a powerful and forceful influence towards the maintenance of world peace.

Harry Truman

Afterward

On August 11, 1945, after Japan still refused to unconditionally surrender, President Truman ordered the military to
drop *Fat Man*, a second atomic bomb, on the Japanese city
of Nagasaki. On August 15, 1945, Japan's Emperor Hiro-
hito announced his acceptance of an unconditional surrender.

Harry S. Truman died on December 26, 1945.

Selected Reading

Ferrell, Robert H., Editor, *The Autobiography of Harry S.
Truman*, 1980.
_____, *Harry S. Truman and the Bomb*, 1996.
McCullough, David, *Truman*, 1992.
Truman, Harry S., *Memoirs*, 1956.
Wainstock, Dennis D., *The Decision to Drop the Atomic Bomb*,
1996.
Walker, J. Samuel, *Prompt and Utter Destruction: Truman and the
Use of Atomic Bombs Against Japan*, 1997.

George Wallace
Segregation Now! Segregation Tomorrow! Segregation Forever!
January 14, 1963

I shall refuse to abide by any illegal, court-ordered integration of Alabama's schools - even to the point of standing in the schoolhouse door.
- George Wallace, March 11, 1962

In 1954 the U.S. Supreme Court, in the landmark *Brown v. Board of Education* decision, struck down as unconstitutional *separate but equal* racial segregation of state-supported schools. Alabama maintained two racially segregated, *separate but equal,* state-supported colleges, the all-white University of Alabama and the all-black Alabama A&M. In 1962 a Federal Court ordered Alabama's colleges integrated.

On June 11, 1963, the date of its court-ordered integration, Alabama Governor George Wallace stood, as he had said he would, blocking the door of the University of Alabama, refusing, for four hours, to allow black students to register - *Mindful of my duties and responsibilities under the Constitution of the United States, the Constitution of the State of Alabama, and seeking to preserve and maintain the peace and dignity of the State, and the individual freedom of its citizens, I denounce and forbid this illegal and unwarranted action by the Federal Government.*

George Corley Wallace, Jr. was born on August 25, 1919 in Clio, Alabama, the child of George, Sr. and Mozelle (Smith) Wallace. Educated at the University of Alabama and the University's Law School, Wallace served in the Alabama Legislature (1946-50), and as a Judge (1950-58), before his 1962 election as a staunch segregationist Governor, proclaiming, *I will stand in the schoolhouse door.*

On January 14, 1963, in Montgomery, Alabama, George Wallace delivered this landmark Inauguration speech, stating his intent to oppose racial integration - *Segregation Now! Segregation Tomorrow! Segregation Forever!*

This is the day of my Inauguration as Governor of the State of Alabama. And on this day I feel a deep obligation to renew my pledges, my covenants with you, the people of this great State.

General Robert E. Lee said that *duty* is the sublimest word in the English language and I have come, increasingly, to realize what he meant. I shall do my duty to you - God helping - to every man, to every woman. . . .

Today I have stood where once Jefferson Davis stood, and took an oath to my people. It is very appropriate then that, from this Cradle of the Confederacy, this very Heart of the Great Anglo-Saxon Southland, that today we sound the drum for freedom as have our generations of forebears before us done, time and again down through history. Let us rise to the call of freedom - loving blood that is in us and send our answer to the tyranny that clanks its chains upon the South. In the name of the greatest people that have ever trod this earth, I draw the line in the dust and toss the gauntlet before the feet of tyranny and I say, Segregation Now! Segregation Tomorrow! Segregation Forever!

The Washington, D. C. school riot report is disgusting and revealing. We will not sacrifice our children to any such type school system - and you can write that down. The federal troops in Mississippi could better be used guarding the safety of the citizens of Washington, D. C., where it is even unsafe to walk or go to a ballgame - and that is the nation's capitol. I was safer in a B-29 bomber over Japan during the war in an air raid than the people of Washington are walking in the White House neighborhood. A closer example is Atlanta. The city officials fawn for political reasons over school integration and then build barricades to stop residential integration - what hypocrisy!

196

Let us send this message back to Washington by our representatives who are with us today that from this day we are standing up, and the heel of tyranny does not fit the neck of an upright man - that we intend to take the offensive and carry our fight for freedom across this nation, wielding the balance of power we know we possess in the Southland - that we, not the insipid bloc voters of some sections, will determine in the next election who shall sit in the White House of these United States. That from this day, from this hour, from this minute, we give the word of a race of honor that we will tolerate their boot in our face no longer. And let those certain judges put that in their opium pipes of power and smoke it for what it is worth.

Hear me, Southerners! You sons and daughters who have moved north and west throughout this nation. We call on you from your native soil to join with us in national support and vote - and we know, wherever you are, away from the hearths of the Southland, that you will respond - for though you may live in the farthest reaches of this vast country, your heart has never left Dixieland.

And you native sons and daughters of old New England's rock-ribbed patriotism, and you sturdy natives of the great Midwest, and you descendants of the far West flaming spirit of pioneer freedom - we invite you to come and be with us, for you are of the Southern mind, and the Southern spirit, and the Southern philosophy. You are Southerners too, and brothers with us in our fight. . . .

Afterward

After George Wallace stepped away from the schoolhouse door, the University of Alabama was integrated without further incident. Wallace served four terms as Alabama's Governor, evolving politically from a staunch segregationist, appealing only to a white constituency, to a true populist, appealing to a multi-racial constituency.

George Wallace died on September 13, 1998.

Selected Reading

Carter, Dan, *The Politics of* Rage, 1995.

Clark, E. Culpepper, *The Schoolhouse Door: Segregation's Last Stand at the University of Alabama*, 1993.

Dorman, Michael, *The George Wallace Myth*, 1976.

Frady, Marshall, *Wallace*, 1976.

Greenhaw, Wayne, *Watch Out for George Wallace*, 1976.

Lesher, Stephan, *George Wallace: American Populist*, 1994.

Wallace, George C., *Stand Up for America*, 1976.

Ryan White
I Have AIDS
March 3, 1988

As much as we've talked to you about AIDS, a lot of you still aren't listening. If someone's trying to get you to have sex or do drugs, before you do something stupid, pick up the phone and call an AIDS hot line. Let's work together to beat AIDS.

- Ryan White, Public Service Announcement, 1989

Ryan White was born on December 6, 1971 in Kokomo, Indiana, the child of Wayne and Jeanne (Hale) White. Ryan, born a hemophiliac, lived in constant danger of bleeding to death. The only treatment for hemophilia was blood transfusions. Donated blood used in transfusions was not then screened for the HIV virus. In 1984 tests confirmed that Ryan, who had received multiple blood transfusions, had AIDS. In the mid-1980's, a diagnosis of AIDS was a death sentence to the patient and a cause of fear and panic to the public. An anonymous letter to the Kokomo *Tribune* started an AIDS panic - *Would you want your little brother to be in school with Ryan White, who constantly threatens to bite, scratch, or spit on other children? How about eating food from a local store where he was spitting on the fresh produce? Or using a restroom where he urinated on the walls?* On July 30, 1985, at the urging of frightened parents and fearful teachers, Ryan was expelled from school. The story of a 13-year-old expelled because he had AIDS made national headlines. Over a year later, when he was re-admitted, almost half of the parents kept their children home. Ryan's family was forced to move.

Ryan began to speak, first locally, and then nationally, about AIDS education and discrimination. Ryan's story was told in a PBS documentary, *I Have AIDS - A Teenager's Story*, and a Hollywood film, *The Ryan White Story*.

On March 3, 1988, in Washington, D.C., in testimony before the President's Commission on AIDS, Ryan White gave this landmark speech, *I Have AIDS*.

Ryan White

My name is Ryan White. I am sixteen years old. I have hemophilia, and I have AIDS.

When I was three days old, the doctors told my parents I was a severe hemophiliac, meaning my blood does not clot. Lucky for me, there was a product just approved by the Food and Drug Administration. It was called Factor VIII, which contains the clotting agent found in blood. While I was growing up, I had many bleeds or hemorrhages in my joints which made it very painful. Twice a week I would receive injections or IVs of Factor VIII which clotted the blood and then broke it down. A bleed occurs from a broken blood vessel or vein. The blood then had nowhere to go, so it would swell up in a joint. You could compare it to trying to pour a quart of milk into a pint-sized container of milk. The first five to six years of my life were spent in and out of the hospital. All in all I led a pretty normal life.

Most recently my battle has been against AIDS and the discrimination surrounding it. On December 17, 1984, I had surgery to remove two inches of my left lung due to pneumonia. After two hours of surgery, the doctors told my mother I had AIDS. I contracted AIDS through my Factor VIII which is made from blood. When I came out of surgery, I was on a respirator and had a tube in my left lung. I spent Christmas and the next thirty days in the hospital. A lot of my time was spent searching, thinking, and planning my life.

I came face to face with death at thirteen years old. I was diagnosed with AIDS - a killer. Doctors told me I'm not contagious. Given six months to live and being the fighter that I am, I set high goals for myself. It was my decision to live a normal life, go to school, be with my friends, and enjoy day-to-day activities. It was not going to be easy.

The school I was going to said they had no guidelines for a person with AIDS. The school board, my teachers, and my principal voted to keep me out of the classroom even after the guidelines were set by the I.S.B.H., for fear of someone getting AIDS from me by casual contact. Rumors of sneezing, kissing, tears, sweat, and saliva spreading AIDS caused people to panic.

We began a series of court battles for nine months, while I was attending classes by telephone. Eventually, I won the right to attend school, but the prejudice was still there. Listening to medical facts was not enough. People wanted one hundred percent guarantees. There are no one hundred percent guarantees in life, but concessions were made by Mom and me to help ease the fear. We decided to meet everyone halfway - separate restrooms, no gym, separate drinking fountain, disposable eating utensils and trays - even though we knew that AIDS was not spread through casual contact. Nevertheless, parents of twenty students started their own school. They were still not convinced. Because of the lack of education on AIDS, discrimination, fear, panic, and lies surrounded me. I became the target of Ryan White jokes. Lies about me biting people. Spitting on vegetables and cookies. Urinating on bathroom walls. Some restaurants threw away my dishes. My school locker was vandalized inside and folders were marked FAG and other obscenities.

I was labeled a troublemaker, my mom an unfit mother, and I was not welcome anywhere. People would get up and leave, so they would not have to sit anywhere near me. Even at church, people would not shake my hand. This brought on the news media, TV crews, interviews, and numerous public appearances. I became known as the AIDS boy. I received thousands of letters of support from all around the world, all because I wanted to go to school.

Mayor Koch of New York was the first public figure to give me support. Entertainers, athletes, and stars started giving me support. I met some of the greatest, like Elton John, Greg Louganis, Max Headroom, Alyssa Milano (my teen idol), Lyndon King (Los Angeles Raiders), and Charlie Sheen. All of these plus many more became my friends, but I had very few friends at school. How could these people in the public eye not be afraid of me but my whole town was?

It was difficult at times to handle; but I tried to ignore the injustice, because I knew the people were wrong. My family and I held no hatred for those people because we realized they were victims of their own ignorance. We had great faith that with patience, understanding, and education, that my family and I could be helpful in changing their minds and attitudes around. Financial hardships were rough on us, even though Mom had a good job at G.M. The more I was sick, the more work she had to miss. Bills became impossible to pay. My sister, Andrea, was a championship roller skater who had to sacrifice too. There was no money for her lessons and travel. AIDS can destroy a family if you let it, but luckily for my sister and me, Mom taught us to keep going. Don't give up, be proud of who you are, and never feel sorry for yourself.

After two and a half years of declining health, two attacks of pneumocystis, shingles, a rare form of whooping cough, and liver problems, I faced fighting chills, fevers, coughing, tiredness, and vomiting. I was very ill and being tutored at home. The desire to move into a bigger house, to avoid living AIDS daily, and a dream to be accepted by a community and school, became possible and a reality with a movie about my life, *The Ryan White Story*.

My life is better now. At the end of the school year (1986-87), my family and I decided to move to Cicero, Indiana.

We did a lot of hoping and praying that the community would welcome us, and they did. For the first time in three years, we feel we have a home, a supportive school, and lots of friends. The communities of Cicero, Atlanta, Arcadia, and Noblesville, Indiana, are now what we call *home*. I'm feeling great.

I'm a normal happy teenager again. I have a learner's permit. I attend sports functions and dances. My studies are important to me. I made the honor roll just recently, with two A's and two B's. I'm just one of the kids, and all because the students at Hamilton Heights High School listened to the facts, educated their parents and themselves, and believed in me.

I believe in myself as I look forward to graduating from Hamilton Heights High School in 1991. Hamilton Heights High School is proof that AIDS education in schools works.

Afterward

On April 8, 1990, Ryan White, eighteen, died of complications from AIDS. Indiana's Governor, calling Ryan *an American hero*, ordered all flags in the state to fly at half-mast. On August 18, 1990, the U.S. Congress passed the Ryan White AIDS Care Act.

Selected Reading

White, Jeanne, with Susan Dworkin, *Weeding Out the Tears: A Mother's Story of Love, Loss and Renewal*, 1997.
White, Ryan, and Ann Marie Cunningham, *Ryan White: My Own Story*, 1991.

Movies:
The Ryan White Story, 1989.

Woodrow Wilson
The League Of Nations
January 25, 1919

Victory would mean peace forced upon the loser, a victor's terms imposed upon the vanquished. It would be accepted in humiliation, under duress, at an intolerable sacrifice, and would leave a sting, a resentment, a bitter memory upon which terms the peace would rest, not permanently, but only as upon quicksand. Only a peace between equals can last, only a peace the very principle of which is equality and common participation in a common effort.

- Woodrow Wilson, January 22, 1917

The Great War or *The War To End All Wars,* now known as the First World War, ended on Armistice Day, November 11, 1918, having caused an estimated 10 million deaths worldwide. The victorious Allied Powers - the United States, Great Britain, and France - met in January 1919 at Versailles, France, to work out the details of a peace treaty with the defeated Central Powers - Germany and Austria-Hungary. Promising the American people, who had suffered over 50,000 battle deaths in the War, that he would work to *make the world safe for democracy,* U.S. President Woodrow Wilson proposed a peace treaty based on *Fourteen Points For Peace,* including the creation of a League of Nations.

Woodrow Wilson was born on December 28, 1856 in Staunton, Virginia, the child of Joseph and Janet (Woodrow) Wilson. Educated at Princeton University, the University of Virginia Law School, and Johns Hopkins University, Wilson spent fourteen years (1886-1910) as a noted educator, rising to the Presidency of Princeton University. In 1910 he was elected Governor of New Jersey and in 1912 President of the United States.

On January 25, 1919, Woodrow Wilson delivered this landmark speech at the Versailles Peace Conference, proposing to avoid future wars by creating *The League Of Nations.*

Mr. Chairman, I consider it a distinguished privilege to be permitted to open the discussion in this conference on the League of Nations. We have assembled for two purposes - to make the present settlements which have been rendered necessary by this war, and also to secure the peace of the world, not only by the present settlements, but by the arrangements we shall make at this conference for its maintenance. The League of Nations seems to me to be necessary for both of these purposes. . . .

We are assembled under very peculiar conditions of world opinion. I may say without straining the point that we are not representatives of governments, but representatives of peoples. It will not suffice to satisfy governmental circles anywhere. It is necessary that we should satisfy the opinion of mankind. The burdens of this war have fallen in an unusual degree upon the whole population of the countries involved. I do not need to draw for you the picture of how the burden has been thrown back from the front upon the older men, upon the women, upon the children, upon the homes of the civilized world, and how the real strain of the war has come where the eye of government could not reach, but where the heart of humanity beats. We are bidden by these people to make a peace which will make them secure. We are bidden by these people to see to it that this strain does not come upon them again, and I venture to say that it has been possible for them to bear this strain because they hoped that those who represented them could get together after this war and make such another sacrifice unnecessary.

It is a solemn obligation on our part, therefore, to make permanent arrangements that justice shall be rendered and peace maintained. This is the central object of our meeting.

Settlements may be temporary, but the action of the nations in the interest of peace and justice must be permanent. We can set up permanent processes. We may not be able to set up permanent decisions. Therefore, it seems to me that we must take, so far as we can, a picture of the world into our minds. Is it not a startling circumstance, for one thing, that the great discoveries of science, that the quiet studies of men in laboratories, that the thoughtful developments which have taken place in quiet lecture rooms, have now been turned to the destruction of civilization? The powers of destruction have not so much multiplied as gained facility. The enemy whom we have just overcome had at his seats of learning some of the principal centers of scientific study and discovery, and he used them in order to make destruction sudden and complete, and only the watchful, continuous cooperation of men can see to it that science as well as armed men is kept within the harness of civilization.

In a sense the United States is less interested in this subject than the other nations here assembled. With her great territory and her extensive sea borders, it is less likely that the United States should suffer from the attack of enemies than that many of the other nations here should suffer; and the ardor of the United States - for it is a very deep and genuine ardor - for the society of nations is not an ardor springing out of fear or apprehension, but an ardor springing out of the ideals which have come to consciousness in this war. In coming into this war the United States never for a moment thought that she was intervening in the politics of Europe or the politics of Asia or the politics of any part of the world. Her thought was that all the world had now become conscious that there was a single cause which turned upon the issues of this war. That was the cause of justice and of liberty for men of every kind and place. Therefore, the United States should feel that its part in this war had been played in vain if there ensued upon it merely a body of European settlements. It would feel that it could not take part in guaranteeing those European settlements unless that guaranty involved the continuous superintendence of the peace of the world by the associated nations of the world.

Therefore, it seems to me that we must concert our best judgment in order to make this League of Nations a vital thing - not merely a formal thing, not an occasional thing, not a thing sometimes called into life to meet an exigency - but always functioning in watchful attendance upon the interests of the nations - and that its continuity should be a vital continuity - that it should have functions that are continuing functions and that do not permit an intermission of its watchfulness and of its labor - that it should be the eye of the nations to keep watch upon the common interest, an eye that does not slumber, an eye that is everywhere watchful and attentive.

And if we do not make it vital, what shall we do? We shall disappoint the expectations of the peoples. This is what their thought centers upon. I have had the very delightful experience of visiting several nations since I came to this side of the water, and every time the voice of the body of the people reached me through any representative, at the front of its plea stood the hope for the League of Nations. Gentlemen, the select classes of mankind are no longer the governors of mankind. The fortunes of mankind are now in the hands of the plain people of the whole world. Satisfy them, and you have justified their confidence not only but established peace. Fail to satisfy them, and no arrangement that you can make will either set up or steady the peace of the world.

You can imagine, gentlemen, I dare say, the sentiments and the purpose with which representatives of the United States support this great project for a League of Nations. We regard it as the keystone of the whole program which expressed our purposes and ideals in this war and which the associated nations have accepted as the basis of the settlement. If we returned to the United States without having made every effort in our power to realize this program, we should return to meet the merited scorn of our fellow citizens. For they are a body that constitutes a great democracy. They expect their leaders to speak their thoughts and no private purpose of their own. They expect their representatives to be their servants. We have no choice but to obey their mandate. But it is with the greatest enthusiasm and pleasure that we accept that mandate; and because this is the keystone of the whole fabric, we have pledged our every purpose to it, as we have to every item of the fabric. We would not dare abate a single part of the program which constitutes our instruction. We would not dare compromise upon any matter as the champion of this thing - this peace of the world, this attitude of justice, this principle that we are the masters of no people but are here to see that every people in the world shall choose its own masters and govern its own destinies, not as we wish but as it wishes. We are here to see, in short, that the very foundations of this war are swept away. Those foundations were the private choice of small coteries of civil rulers and military staffs. Those foundations were the aggression of great powers upon the small. Those foundations were the holding together of empires of unwilling subjects by the duress of arms. Those foundations were the power of small bodies of men to work their will upon mankind and use them as pawns in a game. And nothing less than the emancipation of the world from these things will accomplish peace.

You can see that the representatives of the United States are, therefore, never put to the embarrassment of choosing a way of expediency, because they have laid down for them the unalterable lines of principle. And, thank God, those lines have been accepted as the lines of settlement by all the high-minded men who have had to do with the beginnings of this great business.

I hope, Mr. Chairman, that when it is known, as I feel confident it will be known, that we have adopted the principle of the League of Nations and means to work out that principle in effective action, we shall by that single thing have lifted a great part of the load of anxiety from the hearts of men everywhere. We stand in a peculiar case. As I go about the streets here, I see everywhere the American uniform. Those men came into the war after we had uttered our purposes. They came as crusaders, not merely to win a war, but to win a cause; and I am responsible to them, for it fell to me to formulate the purposes for which I asked them to fight, and I, like them, must be a crusader for these things, whatever it costs and whatever it may be necessary to do, in honor, to accomplish the object for which they fought. I have been glad to find from day to day that there is no question of our standing alone in this matter, for there are champions of this cause upon every hand. I am merely avowing this in order that you may understand why, perhaps, it fell to us, who are disengaged from the politics of this great Continent and of the Orient, to suggest that this was the keystone of the arch and why it occurred to the generous mind of our president to call upon me to open this debate. It is not because we alone represent this idea, but because it is our privilege to associate ourselves with you in representing it.

I have only tried in what I have said to give you the fountains of the enthusiasm which is within us for this thing, for those fountains spring, it seems to me, from all the ancient wrongs and sympathies of mankind, and the very pulse of the world seems to beat to the surface in this enterprise.

Afterward

Choosing to ignore Woodrow Wilson's Fourteen Points For Peace, Britain and France imposed upon Germany the impossibly harsh terms of the Versailles Treaty. In the end, the Allies agreed to only one of Wilson's Fourteen Points, The League of Nations. President Wilson, a Democrat, could not, despite his best efforts, get the Republican-controlled U.S. Senate to agree to join The League of Nations. Without American participation, The League of Nations proved unable to prevent a Second World War. For his efforts, Wilson was awarded the 1920 Nobel Peace Prize.

Woodrow Wilson died on February 3, 1924.

Selected Reading

Ambrosius, Lloyd E., *Woodrow Wilson and the American Diplomatic Tradition: The Treaty Fight in Perspective*, 1987.

Bolling, John Randolph, and Mary Vanderpool Pennington, et al., Compilers, *Chronology of Woodrow Wilson, Together with His Most Notable Addresses, A Brief Description of the League of Nations, and the League of Nations Covenant*, 1927.

Fleming, Denna F., *The United States and the League of Nations*, 1968.

Jacobs, David, *An American Conscience: Woodrow Wilson's Search for World Peace*, 1973.

Knock, Thomas J., *To End All Wars: Woodrow Wilson and the Quest for a New World Order*, 1995.

Stone, Ralph A., Editor, *Wilson and the League of Nations: Why America's Rejection?*, 1967.

Malcolm X
The Ballot Or The Bullet
April 3, 1964

I am willing by any means necessary to bring an end to the injustices our people suffer.
- Malcolm X, 1965

Malcolm Little was born on May 19, 1925 in Omaha, Nebraska, the child of Earl and Louisa (Norton) Little. In and out of trouble with the law, Malcolm Little, at the age of twenty, was sent to a Massachusetts Prison where, in 1948, he converted to a militant black nationalist sect, the Nation of Islam, also called The Black Muslims. Malcolm Little became Malcolm X.

After his release in 1952, Black Muslim Minister Malcolm X preached for the next twelve years in many of the Nation of Islam's mosques, including those in Philadelphia, New York City, Atlanta, Detroit, Chicago, and Los Angeles. As National Spokesperson for the Nation of Islam (1957-64), Malcolm X spoke to black and white audiences alike with the same message - *If America can't atone for the crimes she has committed against the twenty-two million Negroes, if she can't undo the evils she has brutally, mercilessly heaped upon our people these past four hundred years, then America has signed her own doom! (1963) You don't have a peaceful revolution. You don't have a turn-the-cheek revolution. There is no such thing as a nonviolent revolution. Revolution is bloody, revolution is hostile, revolution knows no compromise, revolution destroys everything that gets in its way. (1963) I tell you that the time has come for the black man to die fighting. If he's going to die, let him die fighting. (1964) We declare our right on this earth to be human beings, to be respected as human beings, to be given the rights of human beings in this society, on this earth, in this day, which we intend to bring into existence by any means necessary. (1964)*

On April 3, 1964, at Cleveland, Ohio's Cory Methodist Church, at a symposium sponsored by the Congress on Racial Equality, Malcolm X delivered this landmark speech on race relations in America, *The Ballot or the Bullet.*

It's true we're Muslims and our religion is Islam, but we don't mix our religion with our politics and our economics and our social and civil activities - not any more. We keep our religion in our mosque. After our religious services are over, then as Muslims we become involved in political action, economic action and social and civic action. We become involved with anybody, anywhere, any time and in any manner that's designed to eliminate the evils, the political, economic and social evils that are afflicting the people of our community.

The political philosophy of black nationalism means that the black man should control the politics and the politicians in his own community; no more. The black man in the black community has to be re-educated into the science of politics so he will know what politics is supposed to bring him in return. Don't be throwing out any ballots. A ballot is like a bullet. You don't throw your ballots until you see a target, and if that target is not within your reach, keep your ballot in your pocket. The political philosophy of black nationalism is being taught in the Christian church. It's being taught in the NAACP. It's being taught in CORE meetings. It's being taught in SNCC meetings. It's being taught in Muslim meetings. It's being taught where nothing but atheists and agnostics come together. It's being taught everywhere. Black people are fed up with the dillydallying, pussyfooting, compromising approach that we've been using toward getting our freedom. We want freedom *now*, but we're not going to get it saying *We Shall Overcome*. We've got to fight until we overcome.

The economic philosophy of black nationalism is pure and simple. It only means that we should control the economy of our community. Why should white people be running all the stores in our community? Why should white people be running the banks of our community? Why should the economy of our community be in the hands of the white man? Why? If a black man can't move his store into a white community, you tell me why a white man should move his store into a black community. The philosophy of black nationalism involves a re-education program in the black community in regards to economics. Our people have to be made to see that any time you take your dollar out of your community and spend it in a community where you don't live, the community where you live will get poorer and poorer, and the community where you spend your money will get richer and richer. Then you wonder why where you live is always a ghetto or a slum area. And where you and I are concerned, not only do we lose it when we spend it out of the community, but the white man has got all our stores in the community tied up, so that, though we spend it in the community, at sundown the man who runs the store takes it over across town somewhere. He's got us in a vise.

So the economic philosophy of black nationalism means in every church, in every civic organization, in every fraternal order, it's time now for our people to become conscious of the importance of controlling the economy of our community. If we own the stores, if we operate the businesses, if we try and establish some industry in our own community, then we're developing to the position where we are creating employment for our own kind. Once you gain control of the economy of your own community, then you don't have to picket and boycott and beg some cracker downtown for a job in his business.

The social philosophy of black nationalism only means that we have to get together and remove the evils, the vices, alcoholism, drug addiction, and other evils that are destroying the moral fiber of our community. We ourselves have to lift the level of our community, the standard of our community to a higher level, make our own society beautiful so that we will be satisfied in our own social circles and won't be running around here trying to knock our way into a social circle where we're not wanted.

So I say, in spreading a gospel such as black nationalism, it is not designed to make the black man re-evaluate the white man - you know him already - but to make the black man re-evaluate himself. Don't change the white man's mind - you can't change his mind, and that whole thing about appealing to the moral conscience of America - America's conscience is bankrupt. She lost all conscience a long time ago. Uncle Sam has no conscience. They don't know what morals are. They don't try and eliminate an evil because it's evil, or because it's illegal, or because it's immoral; they eliminate it only when it threatens their existence. So you're wasting your time appealing to the moral conscience of a bankrupt man like Uncle Sam. If he had a conscience, he'd straighten this thing out with no more pressure being put upon him. So it is not necessary to change the white man's mind. We have to change our own mind. You can't change his mind about us. We've got to change our own minds about each other. We have to see each other with new eyes. We have to see each other as brothers and sisters. We have to come together with warmth so we can develop unity and harmony that's necessary to get this problem solved ourselves. How can we do this? How can we avoid jealousy? How can we avoid the suspicion and the divisions that exist in the community? I'll tell you how.

. . . . Our gospel is black nationalism. We're not trying to threaten the existence of any organization, but we're spreading the gospel of black nationalism. Anywhere there's a church that is also preaching and practicing the gospel of black nationalism, join that church. If the NAACP is preaching and practicing the gospel of black nationalism, join the NAACP. If CORE is spreading and practicing the gospel of black nationalism, join CORE. Join any organization that has a gospel that's for the uplift of the black man. And when you get into it and see them pussyfooting or compromising, pull out of it because that's not black nationalism. We'll find another one.

And in this manner, the organizations will increase in number and in quantity and in quality, and by August, it is then our intention to have a black nationalist convention which will consist of delegates from all over the country who are interested in the political, economic and social philosophy of black nationalism. After these delegates convene, we will hold a seminar, we will hold discussions, we will listen to everyone. We want to hear new ideas and new solutions and new answers. And at that time, if we see fit then to form a black nationalist party, we'll form a black nationalist party. If it's necessary to form a black nationalist army, we'll form a black nationalist army. It'll be the ballot or the bullet. It'll be liberty or it'll be death.

It's time for you and me to stop sitting in this country, letting some cracker senators, Northern crackers and Southern crackers, sit there in Washington, D. C., and come to a conclusion in their mind that you and I are supposed to have civil rights. There's no white man going to tell me anything about my rights. Brothers and sisters, always remember, if it doesn't take senators and congressmen and presidential proclamations to give freedom to the white man, it is not necessary for legislation or proclamation or Supreme Court decisions to give freedom to the black man. You let that white man know, if this is a country of freedom, let it be a country of freedom, and if it's not a country of freedom, change it.

We will work with anybody, anywhere, at any time, who is genuinely interested in tackling the problem head-on, nonviolently as long as the enemy is nonviolent, but violent when the enemy gets violent. We'll work with you on the voter registration drive, we'll work with you on rent strikes, we'll work with you on school boycotts. I don't believe in any kind of integration; I'm not even worried about it because I know you're not going to get it anyway; you're not going to get it because you're afraid to die; you've got to be ready to die if you try and force yourself on the white man, because he'll get just as violent as those crackers in Mississippi, right here in Cleveland. But we will still work with you on the school boycotts because we're against a segregated school system. A segregated school system produces children who, when they graduate, graduate with crippled minds. But this does not mean that a school is segregated because it's all black. A segregated school means a school that is controlled by people who have no real interest in it whatsoever.

Let me explain what I mean. A segregated district or community is a community in which people live, but outsiders control the politics and the economy of that community. They never refer to the white section as a segregated community. It's the all-Negro section that's a segregated community. Why? The white man controls his own school, his own bank, his own economy, his own politics, his own everything, his own community - but he also controls yours. When you're under someone else's control, you're segregated. They'll always give you the lowest or the worst that there is to offer, but it doesn't mean you're segregated just because you have your own. You've got to control your own. Just like the white man has control of his, you need to control yours.

You know the best way to get rid of segregation? The white man is more afraid of separation than he is of integration. Segregation means that he puts you away from him, but not far enough for you to be out of his jurisdiction; separation means you're gone. And the white man will integrate faster than he'll let you separate. So we will work with you against the segregated school system because it's criminal, because it is absolutely destructive, in every way imaginable, to the minds of the children who have to be exposed to that type of crippling education.

Last but not least, I must say this concerning the great controversy over rifles and shotguns. The only thing that I've ever said is that in areas where the government has proven itself either unwilling or unable to defend the lives and the property of Negroes, it's time for Negroes to defend themselves. Article number two of the constitutional amendments provides you and me the right to own a rifle or a shotgun. It is constitutionally legal to own a shotgun or a rifle. This doesn't mean you're going to get a rifle and form battalions and go out looking for white folks, although you'd be within your rights - I mean, you'd be justified; but that would be illegal and we don't do anything illegal. If the white man doesn't want the black man buying rifles and shotguns, then let the government do its job. That's all. And don't let the white man come to you and ask you what you think about what Malcolm says - why, you old Uncle Tom. He would never ask you if he thought you were going to say, *Amen!* No, he is making a Tom out of you.

So, this doesn't mean forming rifle clubs and going out looking for people, but it is time, in 1964, if you are a man, to let that man know. If he's not going to do his job in running the government and providing you and me with the protection that our taxes are supposed to be for, since he spends all those billions for his defense budget, he certainly can't begrudge you and me spending $12 or $15 for a single-shot, or double-action. I hope you understand. Don't go out shooting people, but any time, brothers and sisters, and especially the men in this audience - some of you wearing Congressional Medals of Honor, with shoulders this wide, chests this big, muscles that big - any time you and I sit around and read where they bomb a church and murder in cold blood, not some grownups, but four little girls while they were praying to the same god the white man taught them to pray to, and you and I see the government go down and can't find who did it.

Why, this man - he can find Eichmann hiding down in Argentina somewhere. Let two or three American soldiers, who are minding somebody else's business way over in South Vietnam, get killed, and he'll send battleships, sticking his nose in their business. He wanted to send troops down to Cuba and make them have what he calls free elections - this old cracker who doesn't have free elections in his own country. No, if you never see me another time in your life, if I die in the morning, I'll die saying one thing - the ballot or the bullet, the ballot or the bullet.

If a Negro in 1964 has to sit around and wait for some cracker senator to filibuster when it comes to the rights of black people, why, you and I should hang our heads in shame. You talk about a march on Washington in 1963, you haven't seen anything. There's some more going down in '64. And this time they're not going like they went last year. They're not going singing *We Shall Overcome*. They're not going with white friends. They're not going with placards already painted for them. They're not going with round-trip tickets. They're going with one-way tickets.

And if they don't want that nonnonviolent army going down there, tell them to bring the filibuster to a halt. The black nationalists aren't going to wait. Lyndon B. Johnson is the head of the Democratic Party. If he's for civil rights, let him go into the Senate next week and declare himself. Let him go in there right now and declare himself. Let him go in there and denounce the Southern branch of his party. Let him go in there right now and take a moral stand - right now, not later. Tell him, don't wait until election time. If he waits too long, brothers and sisters, he will be responsible for letting a condition develop in this country which will create a climate that will bring seeds up out of the ground with vegetation on the end of them looking like something these people never dreamed of.

In 1964, it's the ballot or the bullet. Thank you.

Afterward

Two weeks after this speech, Malcolm X made a pilgrimage to the spiritual home of Islam, the Holy City of Mecca. Upon his return, he resigned from the radical Nation of Islam and founded his own more orthodox ministry, Muslim Mosque, Inc.

On February 21, 1965, Malcolm X was murdered.

Selected Reading

Breitman, George, *The Last Year of Malcolm X: The Evolution of a Revolutionary*, 1999.

_____, Editor, *Malcolm X Speaks: Selected Speeches and Statements*, 1966.

_____, Herman Porter, and Baxter Smith, *The Assassination of Malcolm X*, 1991.

Carson, Clayborne, *Malcolm X: The FBI File*, 1991.

DeCaro, Louis A., Jr., *Malcolm and the Cross: The Nation of Islam, Malcolm X, and Christianity*, 1998.

Dyson, Michael E., *Making Malcolm: The Myth and Meaning of Malcolm X*, 1995.

Gallen, David, *Malcolm X: As They Knew Him*, 1992.

_____, Editor, *A Malcolm X Reader*, 1994.

Goldman, Peter L., *The Death and Life of Malcolm X*, 1979.

Leader, Edward R., *Understanding Malcolm X: The Controversial Changes in His Political Philosophy*, 1993.

Perry, Bruce, *Malcolm*, 1991.

Wood, Joe, Editor, *Malcolm X: In Our Own Image*, 1994.

Wolfenstein, E. Victor, *The Victims of Democracy: Malcolm X and the Black Revolution*, 1993.

X, Malcolm, with Alex Haley, *The Autobiography of Malcolm X*, 1992.

ALSO AVAILABLE FROM
EXCELLENT BOOKS

LANDMARK DECISIONS OF THE
UNITED STATES SUPREME COURT

The actual text of 64 Landmark Decisions of the United States Supreme Court, carefully edited into non-legalese for the general reader, in 6 volumes.

"Remarkable." - Booklist
"Especially recommended." Midwest Book Review

ABORTION DECISIONS OF THE
UNITED STATES SUPREME COURT

The text of 20 major Abortion Decisions of the United States Supreme Court, published on the anniversary of *Roe v. Wade*, edited for the general reader, in 3 volumes.

"Wherever hands-on interest in abortion law runs high, these three unpretentious paperbacks are a good investment." - Booklist

CIVIL RIGHTS DECISIONS OF THE
UNITED STATES SUPREME COURT

The actual text of all major Civil Rights Decisions of the United States Supreme Court, carefully edited into non-legalese for the general reader, in 2 volumes.

FIRST AMENDMENT DECISIONS OF THE
UNITED STATES SUPREME COURT

The actual text of major United States Supreme Court decisions on Freedom of Speech, Freedom of the Press, and Freedom of Religion, edited for the general reader, in 3 volumes.

EXCELLENT BOOKS ORDER FORM

(Please xerox this form so it will be available to other readers.)

Please send
Copy(ies)

_____ of LANDMARK AMERICAN SPEECHES:
  VOL. I: THE 17TH & 18TH CENTURIES @ $17.95
_____ of LANDMARK AMERICAN SPEECHES:
  VOL. II: THE 19TH CENTURY @ $17.95
_____ of LANDMARK AMERICAN SPEECHES:
  VOL. III: THE 20TH CENTURY @ $17.95
_____ of LANDMARK DECISIONS I @ $17.95
_____ of LANDMARK DECISIONS II @ $17.95
_____ of LANDMARK DECISIONS III @ $17.95
_____ of LANDMARK DECISIONS IV @ $17.95
_____ of LANDMARK DECISIONS V @ $17.95
_____ of LANDMARK DECISIONS VI @ $17.95
_____ of SCHOOLHOUSE DECISIONS @ $17.95
_____ of LIFE, DEATH, AND THE LAW @ $17.95
_____ of OBSCENITY & PORNOGRAPHY DECISIONS @ $17.95
_____ of FREEDOM OF SPEECH DECISIONS @ $17.95
_____ of FREEDOM OF THE PRESS DECISIONS @ $17.95
_____ of FREEDOM OF RELIGION DECISIONS @ $17.95
_____ of THE MURDER REFERENCE @ $17.95
_____ of THE RAPE REFERENCE @ $17.95
_____ of ABORTION DECISIONS: THE 1970's @ $17.95
_____ of ABORTION DECISIONS: THE 1980's @ $17.95
_____ of ABORTION DECISIONS: THE 1990's @ $17.95
_____ of CIVIL RIGHTS DECISIONS: 19th CENTURY @ $17.95
_____ of CIVIL RIGHTS DECISIONS: 20th CENTURY @ $17.95
_____ of THE ADA HANDBOOK @ $17.95

Name: _____

Address: _____

City: _____ State: _____ Zip: _____

Add $1 per book for shipping and handling.
California residents add sales tax.
OUR GUARANTEE: Any Excellent Book may be returned at any
time for any reason and a full refund will be made.

Mail your check or money order to: Excellent Books,
Post Office Box 131322, Carlsbad, California 92013-1322
Phone: 760-598-5069/Fax: 240-218-7601/E-mail: xlntbks@aol.com
Internet Address: EXCELLENTBOOKS.COM